They Left Too Soon

Stories Of Sudden Loss

JERRY H. BALL

AB●LET Publishing

COPYRIGHT

They Left Too Soon
Stories Of Sudden Loss

DEDICATION

This book and project is most sincerely dedicated to my very special daughter Dulcie. In her efforts to help another human being, she paid the ultimate price. She is forever remembered by so many people for her hard work and love of dance, art and horses.

For 19 long years, her story has been waiting to be told and now it is, along with all the others who have impacted my life and left their indelible imprint on me.

This is also for all those who have believed in me and what I stand for and strive to be. It is a tribute to all of you who have so blessed me with your kindness, friendship and caring.

The writing of their stories is certainly in honor of all those who I've mentioned here; for their families and friends and others who were affected by their loss.

And finally I dedicate this to my Lord Jesus, who gives me strength and courage each day, and who is solely responsible for my being able to sustain the strength I've needed throughout all these years as each of these sudden losses have occurred.

Be well and God bless you.

Jerry

TABLE OF CONTENTS

ACKNOWLEDGMENTS

HOW ONE MAN HAS DEALT WITH
A LIFETIME OF TRAUMATIC EMOTIONAL EVENTS

Jerry H. Ball

A Thank You Goes Out:

To my son Kegan, for helping me get this book out to the world. My gratitude for his support and encouragement, and his computer skills and talent, cannot be expressed enough. He is my partner in this project and I look forward to a long career with him along side of me as I continue my writing adventures.

To my family: daughter Ann, my computer and picture helper; my sisters Gail and Laura for their encouragement; my daughter Lindsay for all her enthusiasm; my wife Sally for her help; to my other children Trevor, Cuyler, Eric & Courtney and to a large group of church family and friends who are always there when I need them.

I would also like to thank my manuscript previewers Dr. Allen Paris who went above and beyond with professional advice and my good friends Jaime and Stephanie for their very honest and encouraging opinions of the book. A special thank you to Rachael and Emily; Laurel and Trysta; my special friends at UECU and especially Paula, Ron, Paul & Laurie for their inspirational support of this important project.

Additionally & especially, I am indebted to Pam and Deb for their efforts in procuring information and contacts essential to the book's creation. A special thank you goes to Vee Kalnins who so graciously granted me permission to use one of his photographs that is on the cover of this book.

Floyd, Mariah & Hailey at Prater Photography Studio. And most especially to my new young friend and illustrator Bethany Blankinship whose incredible art blesses the pages of this book.

May this book be an encourager and self-helper in that it hopefully provides some insight as to how one human being not only lived through each difficult experience, but how he was able to move on in his life after each one. We will all face much adversity. So let us stand strong in our faith and reach out to help others in their time of need. "What a beautiful thing, God, to give thanks" Psalms 92:1 - The Message.

Ab•let Publishing

BOOKS TO COME

The Incredible Adventures Of Princess Shelby
And The Magical Little Fairies

The Weather – Tornadoes And Storms In My Life

Emotional Sudden Loss

For more information: www.JerryHBall.com

ABOUT THE AUTHOR

Jerry H. Ball

Jerry has lived in Battle Creek, Michigan most of his life. He attended Delton Kellogg schools; participating in football, basketball, track and golf. He loved the theatre and was in two plays. Graduating in 1967, he continued his love for theatre, acting in two more productions.

Growing up poor, his mother did a great job of raising him and his brother and two sisters. He is still very close to his sister Gail whom he sees often, and enjoys calling his sister Terrie in Ludington, Michigan. In 1959, the family moved out to Fine Lake where Jerry met his best friend Roger. Enjoying lake life, he especially loved water skiing and friendships made.

In 1970, Jerry married Shirley Rooker. Their first child, Trevor, was born in Germany in 1972 while he was in the Army. Witnessing the birth is one of his fondest memories. In 1975, a second child almost came into the world in the front seat of their Oldsmobile. He was once again present as Kegan arrived in Community Hospital. With the quickness of her deliveries, the couple planned home births for Dulcie in 1977 and Cuyler in 1982. A proud daddy successfully delivered both with mid-wives arriving after. Foster parenting 29 children, the last of these, Lindsay, was proudly adopted.

While serving in Augsburg, Germany during the Viet Nam War, Jerry again was in a play, and after a fourth performance, the last two in Munich, a producer asked him to star in "You're A Good Man Charlie Brown." Torn between the honor of being asked, and leaving Germany to go back to the States, home won his heart. He finished his military commitment in Texas and then headed back to Michigan.

While growing up at Fine Lake just northwest of Battle Creek, Jerry enjoyed sports and life at the lake. Many of his fondest memories were here. Asking his dad, Burl, to show him some chords on the guitar, he practiced until his fingers bled that first day. Writing his first song in 1969, he has since written over 80 of them, and had one under contract in Nashville, Tennessee. Four visits there helped him become a better artist.

In 1996, Jerry was devastated by the loss of his daughter Dulcie to an automobile accident. With his faith and strong resolve, he survived emotionally and remembers her fondly.

In 1981, he began a career with the Battle Creek Fire Department. His love of people and being able to help them, made for a perfect match. Retiring in 2004, many of his experiences show up in his writing. He began his own house painting business in 1987 and continues with that today.

1990 was the year Jerry decided to take his love of playing the guitar, accordion and Indian flute more seriously. He began playing at child care centers, festivals and nursing homes. His music program is highly regarded in many Michigan communities. He loves what he does and it shows.

His love of basketball led him to an unusual venture. In 2005, he named himself Fireball 1 and headed out to shoot baskets at as many different basketball hoops around Michigan as he could find. For one year he kept track of the different venues. Five years after his last shot, he revived Fireball 1, deciding this time to shoot every day of the year outside in all kinds of weather; attempting over 150,000 shots and raising money to help burn victims through Kalamazoo's Bronson Hospital burn unit.

Also in 1990, Jerry married Sally Palmiter and added three more children, Eric, Courtney and Ann to his family. He also has 12 grandchildren with two more on the way. After living in Marshall, Michigan for three years, the couple moved back to Battle Creek where they reside today.

Since retiring, Jerry has enjoyed his house painting career, but hopes to retire from painting soon and concentrate on his music and writing. He loves visiting with his oldest sons in Virginia and North Carolina, and daughter in Ohio. The rest of the children are close to home. He also has made two trips to visit a special sister and her children in Nebraska.

He has always loved animals. Usually having a family dog, his real love is for cats. Of the present three, one is 8 pounds, and two brothers are 18 pounds each. In his lifetime, Jerry has also raised horses, guinea pigs and rabbits.

Jerry is a strong Christian believer, and loves contemporary Christian music. He is involved with his church, Hope Church of the Nazarene, and really enjoys the strength and hope that his faith provides him. He feels blessed for the many gifts God has given him, and hopes to continue his music ministry for a very long time.

SUDDEN LOSS IN MY LIFE

A TIME FOR REFLECTION

By Jerry H. Ball

March 6, 2013

Why I am writing this at this time, is not such a surprise. I love creating and putting words down on paper (or computer). And yet it is astonishing at least to me, as to why I didn't seriously sit down and finish what I've tried to do so many times before, a long time ago. We find ourselves in busy-ness and all of us must do a better job of prioritizing things in our lives to get the important stuff done. What is important, should always be recognized by us as something not to wait too long to do. And yet this being one of the most profound and important topics in my life, it took me being reminded of it during a brief conversation with a lovely couple whom I had just finished doing some inside painting for.

As I listened to a mother's story after we had suddenly realized both our families had suffered sudden loss, I could sense in me that I mustn't put this project off any longer. It was a sort of wakeup call telling me; urging me, to realize that time is precious. From my words on these pages, I might be able to bring to a realization that one can truly live through and get beyond the terrible "nothingness" that storms over you when you are suddenly and horrifically blasted by the loss of someone very important to you.

Yet even as I write this, I realize that of the many people in my life that have left so unexpectedly, some are not those closest to me. Events that have shaped this world; that have changed history, also have affected me. So why now, is it so important that I'm still at my computer at 4:18 am on the day after my birthday, not able to fall back to sleep? Maybe it's because This Is Important and I'm supposed to write these thoughts down before I'm not able to. Maybe too, it's because my story of sudden loss needs to be shared with others who also have suffered through it. And just maybe, those who were a part of my life need someone to remember them and to let the world know that they were important.

The look on her face told me volumes, as she recounted the disbelief and extreme sadness of the loss of their precious daughter. As I listened, I was once again brought back to the reality of my own unexplainable; unbelievable; heart wrenching-aching; gut-ripping; life-changing loss of my own daughter all those many years ago, on a curving and slippery country road, on a somewhat sunny afternoon. It was Thanksgiving Day -1996 - around 2:20 pm.

Life presents so many challenges to us, but none is more formidable than losing someone who means a great deal to you. For me, and so many others, the loss of a child goes a huge step further; well beyond all the others I've had to deal with during my now 64 years of life. There's no really good way to describe "The Moment", when your life changes forever. Forever. FOREVER!!!

Yet my life did go on after that unbelievable moment because I chose to face the unspeakable, and realized that my loved ones, especially my other children, desperately needed me to stay strong for them. And it wasn't Just my children, but my wife; ex-wife; the boyfriend; relatives; friends, and all those little dancers, (and big ones too), at the dance studio who suddenly lost their incredible instructor and friend.

You see, each of us will deal with a sudden loss very individually. There is no right or wrong way. Just deal with it. And to say it is hard, does not do justice to your emotions; your suddenly convulsing insides, as you scramble to understand; to believe the unbelievable just happened; to cope with the moment and eventually with the absence of someone who is now gone from you forever on this earth.

Each person in this world leaves an impact on all those around them that they've touched in some way. We all know that. And yet do we really embrace all those persons who are most important to us on a regular basis when they are in fact alive and well and in our very regular lives?

There's no shame in me telling you that I am an extremely busy person; always have been. There was once a time when I held down four jobs at once for about two years (120 hours a week), and still made time for my kids activities. And yet, how did I not find more time for these same children who needed their father more during their growing up years. Should I have slowed down during their most formidable years? Financially I was unable to.

And then, after my emotional conversation at the lovely couple's home was over that afternoon, something kept gnawing at me. I told myself I wanted to do something for them.

Years before, soon after my daughter's passing, her boyfriend and I went into the recording studio and made a CD in her memory called Beautiful Dancer. She was certainly that and much, much more. These were songs he and I had each written for and about her. Less than a year later, and with another sudden loss in my life, we again went into the studio, and recorded a CD single song I wrote called "It Seems They Left Too Soon". I wanted this couple to have copies. Maybe, I thought, the music; the words to the songs, would better help them cope with their loss in some way.

It's always difficult to know whether you might be infringing on someone's grieving process even if it has been years that they've been dealing with it. But recently as I was cleaning my old office, I came across both of those CD projects, and listened to them for the first time in a long, long while. Were there tears as I listened? Yes. As many as there were when I listened 15 years ago? No. Does it help me to deal with my daughter's death by listening to them? Absolutely! So I decided that I'd take a chance in giving them a copy along with a little booklet about my special daughter, to maybe help them on their difficult road to recovery with their loss.

As I knocked on the door, he answered with a smile and welcomed me in. I couldn't stay long, and under the circumstances, wanted my visit to be brief and not impose on them. She seemed very grateful as I handed her the little bag with the two CD's, the booklet, and a little letter explaining how I felt about our losses. Their story touched me. I hoped mine would help them.

We said goodbyes and thank-you, and I left with a heavy heart. But I think it was the right thing to do. Will they possibly contact me again? My thought is probably. People suffering loss tend to need that contact with another who has felt their same pain. It's even more important for parents who lose a child!

As I continued cleaning that office, I needed some reading material for my expected lengthy visit to the Secretary of State office to renew my driver's license. In a small stack of books I had placed on a dresser, I grabbed the one entitled, "Lament For A Son" by Nicholas Wolterstorff. I had forgotten about it and couldn't even remember what it was about. It would do I thought.

Sitting there waiting for my number to be called, I opened that little white book with mountains on the cover . I quickly realized that I was supposed to read it at this time in my life. The writer had lost his son to a mountain. I had lost a daughter to a car. They had lost their daughter in a crash, and had just told me their story.

So now I am sitting here at my desk one hour later, knowing that I should no longer put this writing off. I need to tell you my story. It is about Sudden Loss for me and how I've dealt and deal with this difficult subject.

My life has been filled with many unexpected and sudden changes; many of them far from tragic; just the opposite. I have been blessed with a faithful wife, lots of good children and grandchildren, good health, and a God who loves me and mine beyond anything I could ever ask for. But I've also been the casualty of a multiplicity of sudden losses with people close to me and my family.

There comes a time when that great sadness from Sudden Loss should be shared with others in some way, in order for us to be able to move forward in our own lives and not just dwell in sorrow or hidden feelings. My way; the best way for me, is to write about it.

And that I will now attempt to do. Even though what you'll read will be sad, each person I'm writing about should never be forgotten; even in tragedy; especially in tragedy. For to me, they were all very important people. And even those for whom I did not know personally, but still felt great loss in my life, I need to express those feelings about what those people meant to me.

So now we begin this little book and writing, with the challenge to present all those wonderful people in my life who left us so suddenly and without warning; "a fitting tribute as best I know how". And most importantly, this is for my precious daughter Dulcie; so loved and cherished by so many, I now will give my best effort. "I love you Dulcie".

My hope to all of you is that my story of loss and the sharing of it, might help you in some way with your difficult journey.

* (Many of the names I've used in this book are either not their real names, or just the real first name, to protect and respect the privacy of the deceased', their families and those who were closest to them.)

INTRODUCTION - SUDDEN LOSS

Sudden Loss to me is the instantaneous and/or unexpected death of a human being or animal that has given traumatic and intimate emotional distress to another person. My story; this story, is about those individuals who have suddenly died in a variety of ways and whom have greatly impacted my life.

There are many other people who have died during my lifetime that have had long illnesses or passed away from old age. There are tens of thousands that I have been sad about upon my learning of their death, who I barely knew. They are of course important to me, but they are not in this category. Even though I get emotional at funerals or upon hearing someone's difficult news, nothing affects you like a person you are close to in some way whose life has "suddenly and instantaneously" been taken away.

There are several categories that I put my sudden loss in including family; close friend; acquaintance or classmate; individuals who died while I worked for the fire department, and those outside of these categories, including those who perished at the hands of another and/or evil doers. Each of these people impacted my life greatly – directly or indirectly. Some have touched me who lived and died before I was even born, (holocaust victims). But no matter whom they were and whenever they died, they all left an imprint; they all impacted me, and have left an emotional scar.

Some people will wonder why Bobby Kennedy's shooting death for example, weighs so heavy on my heart. It's because I believed in him. For me, he stood for hope in a dark world. Martin Luther King Jr. too. My co-workers on the fire department who passed away suddenly, hit me hard upon learning of their death. I worked side by side with them. The other victims while I worked on the fire department, also greatly affected me.

Of course, those closest to me – family members and friends will always have, and continue to have the greatest impact in my life, even today; even after many years have passed, and their memory is still very much engrained in my mind. And none has impacted my life more than the loss of my daughter Dulcie, on a chilly Thanksgiving Day afternoon on November 28th, 1996. So my beginning story must begin with her story – a day like no other in my recorded history.

THE BACKPACK

Every person has their own way of handling sudden loss. And all of us must emotionally be able to deal with each episode that happens in our life. So how do you cope with the devastating loss of a loved one; a friend; another human being who is important to you.

Over the course of your lifetime, you will have people who are unexpectedly and instantaneously killed by any number of circumstances. It is so hard to initially comprehend what just happened let alone how you will first process the loss and then over time how it will ultimately affect you. If enough traumatic events happen to you over many, many years, it can take an unbelievable toll on your health and wellbeing emotionally, mentally and physically.

When I worked as a firefighter on the Battle Creek Fire Department, a member of the Defusing team, (a small group of professionals trained to help individuals confront and deal with traumatic events), described what we do with our emotions under stress.

We had just returned from a medical run where a baby had died. The team leader explained that everyone, no matter what their position in life, goes through emotional upheavals; especially emergency service response personnel. He explained that we all have an emotional backpack that we place these events into. For the average person, it might take a lifetime to fill it up. Firefighters, police officers, and ambulance personnel will fill it up much more quickly. And when it is full, sometimes even to overflowing, we need to and must empty it out.

I now realize that by my completing this book and the telling of all my sudden loss stories, I was able to relieve the huge emotional burden in my own life. I was finally able to empty out my own backpack.

VEHICLE ACCIDENT – FAMILY/FRIENDS

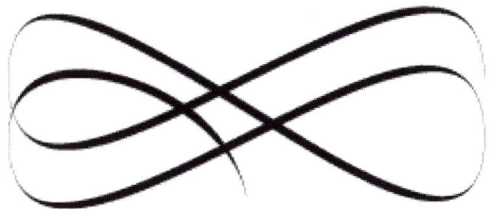

Dulcie Erin Ball - Beautiful Dancer

Dulcie was a five-foot-four bundle of hard work. She did everything at 100%, including and most dynamically, her dancing. At age three, her mother and I introduced her to the world of dance through Shari Rarick's incredible dance studio. So serious was she, even at that young age, of learning her craft well. Over the next 16 years, she thrived on the hard work; reveled in the art of creating, and blossomed into a most amazing dancer and later an instructor.

In school, Dulcie was the epitome of what every teacher dreams their students to be. She would always finish her homework without being asked. In high school, she was always on the honor roll. Even though she was not as gifted as some kids, her hard work helped her accomplish the goal. Switching from Harper Creek to Battle Creek Central in the tenth grade, she continued to excel; joining the pom pon squad; active member of the school newspaper as a writer and on the editing staff. She played softball and ran track as well as participated in choir and band. But her true love was dance.

During her early years in school, she met Jaime Moore who became her best friend during the elementary years. Because of their friendship, years later in 2006, Jaime and I began singing and performing together. Dulcie loved people, and one of her dearest friends was an exchange student from Africa for one year. Dulcie's smile was almost always evident, unless you tried to carry on a conversation early in the morning right after she had awakened for the day.

She performed as part of the competition team at the dance studio, and loved being a part of the chorus line during the annual dance recital at W.K. Kellogg Auditorium in Battle Creek each June. She began teaching dance and adored helping the little dancers be the best they could be. Watching her teach was simply amazing! The consummate encourager, her students and their parents loved and respected her.

Dulcie loved holidays and being with family. She was very close to all of us. She loved horses and riding, and was a decent artist, finishing a self-portrait that each family member has a copy of hanging on their walls. She loved the freedom of adulthood. A year at Western Michigan University and then an apartment in Battle Creek. Life was good.

It was chilly that Thanksgiving morning. She and I talked on the phone for a few moments, making plans for her visit with us later that day. My wife Sally and I and three of the kids would be having our dinner at my mom and dad's house at Fine Lake about 15 miles northwest of Battle Creek. Sometime after 2 pm, with her boyfriend driving Dulcie's little burgundy Corsica, they turned onto 6 Mile road for the short journey to her mother's house for dinner.

The roads were kind of glossy in spots where tree limbs blocked the hazy sun. It was bitey cold in the shade, but tolerable in the sun. As they rounded a curve to the right, they noticed a car had slid off the road and down into a yard on their right, and had come to a stop. They could see a young woman slumped over the steering wheel, so Dulcie had her boyfriend turn the car around and park it on the opposite side of the road where there was a wider shoulder.

Before cell phones were prevalent, and after inspecting the scene, her boyfriend suggested that she go up to the property owner's house to call 911. As she turned to go, a second vehicle driven by a young man one day removed from his military service obligation, was just out for a nice afternoon drive. For some unknown reason, his car went off the road, nearly following the exact wheel prints of the young woman's car, and at the last second was able to swerve to the left – missing the stopped vehicle. That's when his car struck my daughter.

I received the horrible news from my ex-wife while still at my parent's house; that there had been a terrible accident with Dulcie. Of course I tried to focus on the belief that it couldn't be that bad; that I would be able to somehow arrive at the hospital and my injured daughter would hold my hand and I somehow could make it alright. They wouldn't let me or the family in at first, but finally the doctor agreed we could see her.

So cold was her face. So still. So not like my Dulcie. How could this be? I just stared at her lifeless face and held her cold, pale left hand. There were family members all around by now; everyone falling apart.

4

A neighbor was who called my ex-wife. She and my daughter Lindsay hurried down to the accident scene shortly after it happened. Now here they were in this dark hospital room. Dulcie's boyfriend; my son Cuyler; my wife Sally; her mom's husband were all there. Uncontrollable sobbing and weeping and disbelief and horror and crushing, agonizing, stabbing gut wrenching emotions filled this space. Our precious Dulcie was gone.

I walked into the house stunned!!!! I felt lifeless and helpless and yet had to remain strong for the rest of the children and my wife. I felt dead inside. Hollow. Disillusioned. In a fog. I couldn't figure out what to do with myself. Sit down; stand up; wander, in circles, aimlessly around the house I went, then finally walked down the basement stairs to a bedroom there to try and make some sense of it all. There was no sense to it all I thought. Was there someone to blame? Who should it be? Through it all, I never blamed God!

I had to let her brothers know. I had just talked to Trevor in Virginia that morning. Such a cheery conversation. I needed to call Kegan in Illinois. I left him a message on his voice mail. The tone and emotion for the second call to Trevor was heart crushing and devastating.

Sit down; stand up; repeat; repeat; repeat. Finally I pulled myself together and picked up a yellow legal pad and began writing; the thing I do best under stress. And I began to write a tribute to my very special daughter. It would be one of the most difficult readings I've ever attempted, but I just knew I needed to say these words at the funeral. She must never be forgotten. Her friends; the family; church family; others – all needed to know a little more about her.

Sunday, the 31st was visitation at the Henry Funeral Home in Battle Creek. Hundreds filed into the large room throughout a long day that would begin at 10 am and finish just after 10 pm. People from all walks in Dulcie's life. Dancers; family; friends; classmates, acquaintances all paid their respects. All were saddened by their individual loss. All were so kind to the family. Tomorrow would be hard. It would be the hardest day of my life.

Hundreds showed up at North Avenue Church of God – Dulcie's church, on Monday for the funeral and tribute. Music played; words spoken; three special pastor's remarks; tears and sadness; hugs and remembering. My fire lieutenant got permission to lead the funeral procession with Battle Creek Fire Pumper #4. Traveling slowly through the streets in town and then along Beckley Road to Newbre cemetery in Emmett Township, where my daughter would be laid to rest. Even though the sun was out under a clear sky, it was bitterly cold on this first day of December, 1996.

I could barely stand with all of the emotions of the moment. It is so hard to listen to the final brief tribute to my daughter; my Dulcie. Her final tribute, to all in attendance; a loved one; a dear friend. This moment was intensely more difficult; bordering on unbearable, than any I'd ever had before. As I shivered in the cold, we all said our final good-byes. Many family members and close friends stayed a little while. And then the time had come to leave.

There was time to reminisce at the funeral luncheon at the church following the service at the cemetery. A lot of pictures and flowers displayed helped ease the tension and disbelief that filled this place.

After a long while, the people began to leave. Many hugs were given. Many words of encouragement were spoken. Many honest and hurting looks were shared by everyone. And then it was time to go home – with an emptiness I'd never felt before. A "disbelief fog" had clouded the previous four nights. This would be our first realistic night without her.

There was so much to do following the events of the last four days. Putting our emotions back in order would be a priority. For me, I would push myself to go to my December scheduled nursing home visits; struggling to make it through my music program for the residents, but knowing it was one sure way I could emotionally survive my loss. Some of the immediate family secluded themselves from the world. Some just made it through the next day as best they could. Everyone is different. All of us remained sullen for a very long time. Would time heal THIS?

It's only been a few days since I shared the story of my daughter to the couple I had painted for. Their daughter's story touched me deeply and helped resurface my desire to write once again. Dulcie's story needs to be shared. I pray that many will be touched by the wondrous young woman that she was, and the selfless deed to help another person that ended in the loss of her life.

Our Dulcie will always be missed greatly by all those who knew her. The dance studio dedicates one dance each year at the recital in her memory. The Christmas dance performance is also in her name. Her dream of owning her own dance studio will of course, never be realized. But her sister Lindsay, a beautiful dancer in her own right, and an amazing dance instructor, plan to carry on with her dream.

Whenever someone asks, "why did this have to happen to such a good person as she", I'll remind them that it is most biblical to lay down your life for another. She did the right thing. God was there with her, even in this tragedy. A scholarship fund in her memory carries on her work of training dance teachers. Her niece was named after her and at three years old, has already taken to the dance floor with a passion.

As for me, her father, how am I you might ask? I'm well. I'm busy. I love life; my God; my family; my friends, and a goodness that is amongst the darkness and sometimes tragedy of this world. I will always cherish my daughter in memory. I will always remind others in a gentle way, of just how special she was, and how special all of my children and grandchildren are to me. Nothing is more important!

What I've described here is but a few brief moments in the life and then passing away of Dulcie Erin Ball. She was not to be the first tragedy in my life, and many more would follow. As we grow older, there is always a chance that others very close to us will suddenly be gone in an instant. Sudden Loss has no favorites. And yet I am proud of my resilience in dealing with so many losses that have happened in my lifetime.

I would now like to give tribute to those whom I have had the privilege of knowing; some closer than others, who were suddenly gone from my life. The intent is only to share a glimpse of each person's

7

tragedy without painful details. Sudden Loss is never nice. And yet my healing will be made much easier by my telling to others, their ending story.

To Give The Ultimate Sacrifice

We try to teach our children the value of helping others. Chris could think of no better way to spend his life than doing just that. After graduation, he began pursuing in earnest, a career that was spawned in his mind many years before. He wanted to be a firefighter and was completing the training he would need to become one. He was a classmate of my daughter Dulcie; a well-mannered and hardworking young man who like my daughter, had a lot of drive and determination.

In his younger years, I coached Chris in junior league baseball at Wattles Park. I really enjoyed his presence on the team. He was so in tune to helping others. And like my daughter just a few months before; driving down the road with someone he loved, he also stopped along the side of the road to help another motorist in need. He was totally unaware of the danger approaching.

We have expectations and hopes and dreams for our children. His family was so proud of Chris and his aspirations for a career like very few others. Firefighters get to do things that others can only dream of. And now he was so close to fulfilling his dream. Not too long from this particular spring day would he be not just a student of the job, but actually performing the duties that every firefighter revels in. He would be helping people.

That mindset was fully at work as he passed by the car on the side of the busy freeway he was driving on. Chris just had to stop and see if he could be of any assistance. Because he was so focused on the vehicle he was now approaching on foot, he never saw the semi-tractor swerving over just a little to its right. He never had a chance to get out of the way.

The news hit me hard. So similar to my own daughter's accident. So soon afterwards. He was the same age, and attempting to do the same thing in his final moments that she was in hers. Isn't it just so ironic that we can attempt to do good works for others, and tragedy might just be around the corner. I'm sure Chris' parents were proud of him even at his last; especially at the last. He was a fine example for others to follow. He was a blessing to all who knew him.

A Quiet Walk ... And Suddenly

She loved her family so much. Living at St. Mary's lake was wonderful. It made enjoying the out of doors so easy. Water activities and playing in the yard with the children. Taking long walks along quiet country roads during the day when there's very little traffic. Life was good for this young woman. This year she decided to coach her daughter on the softball team in the Wattles Park organization. She knew it would be fun for all the girls. She didn't know a lot about the game, but was willing to give it her best shot. My daughter would be on the same team.

Courtney really loved her coach. The game was fun! The woman was probably thinking about all these things as she and her two little companions were casually walking along the curving and hilly country road near the lake. She suddenly heard the sound of a motorcycle. The lake residents had complained about one cyclist who would ride too fast around their shoreline, but he wouldn't listen.

In a moment the sound was growing louder. Something bothered her but she couldn't put a finger on it. It was such a beautiful sunny day and she was having so much fun walking with her little daughter and the child she babysat for. How could she have known that a real danger was closing in on the three of them.

The woman dearly cared for her family. Every day seemed an adventure. Their life was good. With the softball season in full swing, the ever present smile on her face on the diamond showed how much she enjoyed being out there with her daughter and all the girls. They hadn't won a lot of games so far, but the girls were trying hard and having a good time.

As the three walkers slowly made their way along the roadway, they approached a hill and continued on, step by little step. They didn't need to hurry. There was all the time in the world. It was such a joy for her to be around the children. The sound of the motorcycle was now very loud but it wasn't in sight. Now an uneasy feeling began to grab her in the stomach. She just knew it was that same boy they had told to slow down.

In life we must be ready for the unexpected. How could she have been ready for this however. At over 100 miles per hour, the motorcycle flew over the hill in front of them, and went airborne. Instinctively, she pushed the children out of harm's way. But there was no time for her to jump for safety. She had saved the children, but could not save herself.

Reflections

The intimacy of your feelings for those you are closest to, provides the ultimate devastation to your emotions. My lovely daughter. My child's classmate and one whom I'd coached in baseball. An incredible woman who loved children and died saving two. Internally I was devastated, distraught to the maximum and in shock..

IN MEMORY OF
The Sharing of Sudden Loss
By Jerry H. Ball
March 1, 2013

Today I thought again of what you said.
The terrible loss;
Our sharing the stories,
And feeling the pain.
There's pictures to remember them by,
And thoughts of better times long before
That Day.

So here I am sharing another's grief,
And it hurts me to know you hurt.
If I may, please accept this simple gift of song
To ease a little of the pain.
Our Dulcie was so special!
Your daughter was so special!!
All the children of sudden loss
Deserve to be remembered like a wondrous song
And a sweet poem of life's blessings;
Telling of and reminding us just how much
They've meant to us
And to all who knew and loved them.

Thank you for sharing your story.
I know first-hand how you feel.
I understand your grinding loss.
So I hope and pray that this music –
These songs -
Will be meaningful
And comforting to you.

God bless you always.

Jerry H. Ball

VEHICLE ACCIDENT – HIGH SCHOOL CLASSMATES

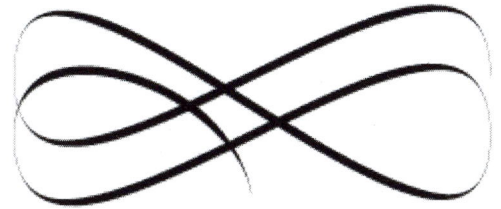

High School Locker Partner And Friend

My family and some friends and I were outside of my house at Fine Lake enjoying the early evening together. The day had been a pleasant one. As we were talking, one of our neighbors, a schoolmate of mine, came up to us and said that there had been a bad accident on Banfield Road. This is a country road with lots of little hills, curves and dips that can be deceiving to your eyes and your perception. I immediately jumped in my car and headed east; with the thought that maybe I could help in some way.

As I approached the scene, multiple vehicles with flashing lights were already there. Walking around, I came upon a body partially covered but with the person's face showing. I didn't recognize him. The girl, who was driving, was still pinned in the car. And the only person I thought I recognized of the seven who were in the car on impact, was another girl sitting against a tree.

Mike was my locker mate and friend, although we didn't spend a lot of time together in school. He had a slight build and probably stood five foot eight and 130 pounds. Nearly always, he had a smile on his face and he really enjoyed the other classmates around him. He and I were both in the main student body stream, and not the so-called "popular crowd". He liked school, the teachers and was a nice guy to be around.

As the evening turned into night, with no moon shining, the vehicle lights made seeing clearly, difficult and a little deceptive. I took another look at the injured driver still pinned; feeling a sadness inside me. There was nothing I could do here, so around 9:30 pm, I decided that it was time to go.

Arriving back home, I filled my mom and dad in on the situation. It troubled me that I couldn't place a name on the girl I recognized. Yet I was sure I knew her. Concentrating on my thoughts of the accident, I wondered who the other six were, including the passenger who had perished.

Several days later at school, they told us that one of our classmates had been killed in a car accident. Why I hadn't recognized Mike I don't know. Come to find out, the driver was a close friend of mine along with her brother. The girl I thought I knew, I didn't. She was from another school.

As they headed for Battle Creek to see a movie that early evening, they came up over a hill and the car they were riding in, slammed into a parked truck sticking out in their lane with no tail lights on. They had no chance to miss it. The driver had a long rehab enabling her to walk again. The other five moved on after the accident.

Backing Out - The Unforeseen

It was most interesting the first time my sister Gail introduced me to her English speaking friend, Hal. He was very polite in his speaking to me and shook my hand with confidence. I knew immediately that I liked him. We hit it off right away. He rode a different bus to school than we did. On this particular morning, he got a ride with a friend of mine and sat happily in the back of her little Volkswagen Beetle. As they backed out of the driveway onto the hilly country road, everything seemed perfect. Sometimes timing is everything. No one saw the yellow school bus that was traveling at a high rate of speed about ready to fly over the hill.

Hal was in a rock & roll band, and I thought that was really cool. It would be another year before I learned to play a guitar on my Dad's old Harmony.

He invited me to one of the band's practices and honored me by making me the new manager after an argument sent the old one away for all of a day.

My sister and he were the same age, and Hal's sister Cindy, was really neat. So I had two reasons to hang around their family. Once, he forgot during a conversation with me, and used his normal voice – no English accent. It didn't matter. Hal was special!

Our bus driver had already been cited before for speeding while driving the route. No one knows if he was behind schedule on this morning. As he crested the hill, the little vehicle with four unsuspecting passengers inside, were carrying on a quiet conversation. The driver of the car had just backed out and came to a stop; then put it in forward; right when the horrendous collision occurred. The bus literally smashed into the back of the little car and the momentum caused the bus to ride up on top of it. The pileup went off the roadway and down into a ditch. No one on the bus was injured. Hal was killed instantly.

We all have special gifts. Hal was one of those people who brought a lot of joy to all those around him. His dry humor and gentle smile made him a favorite whenever he was with friends or around people he didn't even know.

There was great sorrow at the funeral as everyone in attendance knew they had lost a very special young man and friend. Because of who he was, his imprint on the lives of so many will never be erased.

Of Dreams And Sudden Endings

He was a great golfer. Almost made the Michigan State golf team in his first year. To pay for his schooling, he worked two jobs on top of doing his studies. One of those jobs was working at Speed's restaurant during the evening and/or night shift. He was literally wearing himself out, but felt he had to maintain this pace if he was going to make a go of it in college.

On a warm evening after working until around 2 am, Terry left the restaurant in Verona, just east of downtown Battle Creek. It was a dark night and with being so tired following a long night at work, it's easy to kind of find yourself in a haze. A long and hilly back country road with probably no oncoming traffic this time of night. So easy it would be to doze off – just for a moment.

Terry was a really hard worker and had considered becoming a professional golfer. He had very realistic goals for himself, and a quality education at MSU would go a long way towards a regular career should he not make the pro circuit. A quiet young man, his ambition was clearly one of his strong points. He also played a good game of ping pong. Never talking a lot when we were together playing either sport, we both enjoyed the time together.

There are a lot of bodies of water in Barry County that create fog or mist on a warm night. Along Uldricks Drive, there are several places where the road not only is curvy, but has dips and slants to the side here and there.

As he approached a mild right curve, the long and tiring hours must have caught up with him. It only takes a moment sometimes to let your heavy eyelids slip shut – just for a moment you say to yourself. I'm alright. I'm okay. I'm............ .

Terry's car never even started to make the curve. A mammoth 100+ year old oak tree graced the side of the road but maybe eight feet off the shoulder. They figured the impact at 80 miles per hour at a distance of only eight feet was beyond catastrophic! Head on at that speed, the now mass of crumpled and twisted metal actually moved the base of this enormous tree 6 inches.

Everyone around Fine Lake where Terry lived and grew up, were deeply saddened by the young man; friend and brother; and especially son, whose life was so abruptly taken from him. He was genuinely one of the best people anyone around had known. His memory will be long lasting.

A Doctor's Son - A Shining Star

There are people in our life's journey that we have ties too but have never met. Such was the case with my doctor's son, Julian. He was a bright young man with a good future awaiting him. He liked school and loved his family very much. His parents were able to provide for him very well, and he was the type of child who appreciated it.

On this particular day, his dad picked him up after school sometime around the 3 o'clock hour. The sky was a clear blue. They had both taken this same route many times before without incident. But this day would be very different! For coming over a hill was a car with a driver in it who forgot his responsibilities while being on the road. Innocence on this day would be suddenly and tragically taken away.

The family loved being together and doing things. With dad being a doctor, he was always busy. But as much as possible, he would diligently provide the support his family needed not only financially, but emotionally and physically. The children were paramount to both parents.

There was casual conversation going on between father and son. There was no way either of them could have suspected the danger that was about to be sprung on them. We always talk about drinking and driving; how we need tougher laws to combat the problem. Yet how serious are we when we don't take the actions we need to, to change the environment? When will innocent lives taken finally be enough to make us stand up and tolerate the unthinkable happening to our loved ones no longer?

As they were about to pass a side street, the speeding car made little or no effort to stop as it slammed into the front passenger-side of the doctor's vehicle. There was absolutely no time to avoid the collision.

21

There was no time to change anything. There was no time to say "good-bye"!

I hate drunk driving and drunk drivers. I've always told my children as they came of driving age, that if they ever get put in jail for D.D, to call me and let me know that you're okay and, have a nice visit in jail. If you kill someone, I'll still love you because you are my child. But for my child, or anyone else, I Will Not Be Sympathetic in any way to what you have just done and the irreparable damage you've caused to the loved ones whose lives you've just shattered!!! There Is No Excuse that makes this better!!!!!!

Reflections

When I found out that each had suddenly and violently died, my emotions were all cloudy. I had seen two of them just days before. One I had played golf and ping pong with. One was my favorite doctor's son. Just so hard to believe that they were gone.

A Personal Glimpse of...
Terry Teller – A Nice Friend

Some of my fellow classmates at Delton Kellogg high school seemed to blend into the long hallways. And around Fine Lake where we both lived, Terry Teller was not seen outside much other than when he would be loading his golf clubs into the back of his car getting ready to head out for another splendid round of golf. He was also a good ping pong player whom I had the privilege of playing on occasion. But his first love was always for the game of legends – to play golf.

Terry had aspiration of becoming a professional golfer. Locally, his game was one of the best. He once set the Maple Hills golf course record of 59 shooting a 28 on his first trip around the beautiful 9-hole course. Finishing his high school golfing career at the top of his game, he graduated with high honors – good enough to land him entrance into Michigan State University and in invitation as a preferred walk-on for the golf team. He didn't make the team that first year, but his resolve to be successful never wavered. He was determined to be successful at the next level whatever it would take.

His family was a close knit unit and was so encouraging towards Terry and his golfing aspirations. Such a nice young man everyone would tell his mother. He certainly was. The family who with limited resources could only fund part of his college expenses. So he worked two jobs to make ends meet. In addition, he worked part time at local courses to allow him extra playing time to perfect his craft.

Even though we took two very different paths following high school, I will always have fond memories of a young man who worked extremely hard to try and fulfill a dream to one day play on the Professional Golf Tour.

Was he good enough was yet to be determined. With his work ethic and positive attitude and talent, there was no doubt in most people's minds that he had a real shot at it.

VEHICLE ACCIDENT – LOCAL/FRIEND

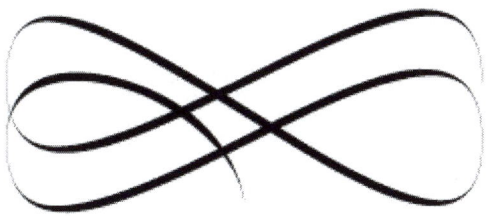

Texting To The End

On a clear afternoon in Battle Creek, a mother was driving down Michigan Avenue just a block from my house. She was heading west and decided she needed to contact her son. Her small car suddenly swerved to the right and struck the curb; causing the vehicle to go airborne and then flip over, right into a mechanic shop's driveway. Not having her seatbelt on, she was thrown from the car, which ended up on top of her.

Several of the workers rushed out and picked up the vehicle and pulled her out. Still alive, but critically injured, she told a rescuer that she was just texting her son. She died shortly after while still on the scene. I've tried to instill in my children how dangerous it is; how preoccupied you are when texting and driving at the same time. I hope they've truly listened.

The law states that texting while driving is dangerous and illegal. But a tremendous number of people still do it. A video from England showed what can happen in a re-creation by actors. It was shown in the United States and there was an uproar. How could you show something like that on TV? Many of those same people were texting their response.

Good Deed Gone Horribly Wrong

It was a beautiful partly cloudy day. A little bit cool in late summer. Just right for doing yard work. Her neighbor had been unable to mow his lawn for quite a while, so she decided that she would cut it for him. Besides, it's enjoyable to cut grass while riding on a lawn tractor she thought.

Traffic is usually light most of the time on this back country road just northwest of Marshall, Michigan. And yet there are times when the garbage trucks fly by en route to the local landfill. Otherwise, it's pretty quiet around there. The front yard is probably 150 feet plus from the house to the road. She was mowing only about 20 feet away from the house when a dump truck driver lost control and careened up into the yard.

She didn't see it coming. No one could ever have imagined it. And how could she, on a moving tractor, and he in a runaway truck have crossed the exact path as one another? And yet they did! The pain for the family was immense! The probability of it ever happening in the first place is beyond imagination. Why these strange things happen, no one is ever able to explain. That's because there is no explanation. We should live each day well, knowing that each one is truly a gift. Don't take your life for granted.

So Small And So Sudden

He was a good friend. All furry and curly and white, little Rocky was a miniature dog whom my daughter Lindsay adored. He, along with her other small dog, Lily, were her companions long before her daughter was born. They were both good watchdogs, and brought a lot of joy to her world.

One night while I was babysitting my wonderful granddaughter Dulcie, in their house in Marshall, Michigan, we were having a lot of fun when suddenly a large bat appeared flying over our heads and doing what bats do best; flying from one room to the next and back, trying to find a way out of the house.

With Dulcie terrified, and me trying but not finding a bad mitten or tennis racket to help knock it down in flight, I decided the best way to eliminate this problem was to open up the front door. Bats will eventually notice the opening, and fly out.

As Dulcie and I sat huddled on the couch, the bat circled the living room; headed back down the hall to the kitchen, and then back down the hallway and out the front door. Excitedly, Dulcie and I quickly closed the door behind the bat's exit.

So relieved, and then suddenly, I heard the screeching of tires and a loud, high pitched yelp. Quickly opening up the door again, I could see a car stopped right in front of the house. And then, almost instantaneously, a second car slammed on its brakes and a final yelp and then nothing. I could see something white in the middle of the road and said it out loud, "Oh no; Oh No!"

I told Dulcie to stay in the house. She watched out the front window as I walked out into the street and gently picked up the little white dog that my daughter so loved. Both cars drivers felt terrible. I thanked them for stopping. Carrying Rocky behind me so Dulcie couldn't see, I placed him in a container on the porch and went back inside.

Sudden loss of a pet can be extremely difficult to emotionally get over. I had to tell my daughter quickly. When she returned home, I broke the news to her. She emotionally was broken hearted. I was so sorrowful. It wasn't my fault, but she had left me in charge of the household including the two dogs, and I felt I had let her down. He was given a quiet burial.

Reflections

Disbelief surfaced for me when I heard of a runaway truck and a totally unsuspecting victim. And then I witnessed firsthand, a "just happened" car accident that was caused by the distraction of texting while driving. My level of all emotions went even higher when my daughter's precious pet dog was suddenly no more.

ACCIDENT

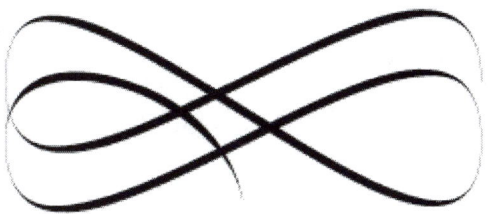

A Daughter's Friend - Unknown Danger

Sometimes in life, we are oblivious to certain people in our immediate surroundings. A young girl in my daughter Dulcie's class, was one of those for her. Like most 12 year olds, the girl liked playing outside with her friends. Most days would be totally uneventful. Most days would just be what you might call normal, whatever normal is for that person.

In a nearby yard to the house where the young girl was staying, a lumber company truck driver had unloaded a tall stack of wooden rafters that would be used to build a garage. Many times with these deliveries, the framing material isn't perfectly balanced on the ground, and could tip or fall under the right circumstances. It seemed like the perfect place for two 12 year old girls to play on and explore. How could they have known that there's always potential danger when construction materials are stacked that high.

The area where this girl was visiting, was one in which many small dwellings existed. It was a quiet neighborhood with lots of children who would get home from school and want to play outside. On weekends, the yards all around the area would see many of those children spending hours playing games and looking for exciting things to do.

The two girls were intrigued by the tall stack of wood in front of them. It almost looked like a good play fort for them to crawl into, onto and over and back. But as they climbed over and under the long expanses of two by sixes and two by eights, an uneasiness came over the girls. One of them climbed out from under the huge structure. The second was on her way out, when something shifted, and in a split second; with no warning, the lumber came tumbling down on top of her small, frail body. In just a moment in time, what had been an adventure with laughter and excitement, became a nightmare for a young girl who could do nothing to help her friend.

Dulcie asked if I would attend the funeral with her. It was a solemn event for the two of us. Dulcie was saddened by the prospect that one of her classmates would never be in school again. She tried to grasp what had happened to her. How could this have happened to someone she knew? These questions arise in all of us in times of trauma and grief. Our lives moved on. But for my daughter, the questions remained. That's why we must live like there's no tomorrow, and yet believe in tomorrow's possibilities. And have a faith in God to help us through the difficulties.

It Seems They Left Too Soon

There's an excitement when the adrenaline rush of doing something a little dangerous is right in front of you. For Jason, he was thrilled to prepare to climb another mountain; to place his skills and confidence to work. An experienced climber, who was definitely in his element, he proceeded to get everything out of his vehicle that he would need for the climb and decent.

Climbing alone is definitely dangerous, and yet he loved the quiet; the solitude that the mountain afforded him from his normal everyday life. The day seemed perfect. The mountain beckoned him. How could anything go wrong with perfect weather and a seasoned veteran climber having all day to enjoy God's creation. But it's what awaited him; that unexpected unknown that was ready to change everything in the lives of all who knew him.

The Olmsted family has always been very active. Living near the beautiful waterways of a Washington State they adored, afforded them the experiences of seeing nature at it's finest. And mountains too; what more could an adventurer ask for. For Jason, life at this time could have been no better. Good family, friends and a sport that few were better at than he.

The climb was near perfect, and so Jason decided to enjoy every minute of the experience for as long as he could. Knowing that climbing late in the day can be dangerous, especially alone, he finally decided that he'd better get down to where his vehicle awaited him. He probably didn't realize how exhausted he was. It had been such a perfect day. How could anything go wrong now. He was so tired.

34

Though much lower than the height he had reached earlier in the day, he was still a long way from the bottom of the majestic mountain. A curving; twisting and dangerous road lie ahead on his journey home. He was so tired. Sometimes when you're tired to the extreme, you aren't as quick with your reflexes as normal. It's hard to keep focused on the task at hand. It's getting dark and not as easy to see the road as clearly as normal. Jason didn't realize the sharp curve to the left was right in front of him. The mountain he so loved would now be his final resting place.

I would write and then record the song, "It Seems They Left Too Soon", shortly after my Aunt Tina called me with the devastating news. It is a tribute to all those who are victims to Sudden Loss.

The Song Of Life Was He

In the music industry, there are a few individuals whose expertise exceeds the norm. Kevin was not only a quality engineer, he was a fantastic musician and singer; a voice teacher, and a great Christian friend. He absolutely loved recording others at his in-home studio in Portage, Michigan.

We first met when I wanted to record some new songs I had recently completed. Years later, Kevin and his wife moved into a huge, newly renovated apartment that was part of a downtown building restoration, that also housed his new world class recording studio.

He took great pride in being able to do a lot of the upgrades to the studio himself. One afternoon when he was not recording anyone, he climbed a tall step ladder to reach up towards the ceiling. Maybe it was his balance that was off a bit. Maybe it was an unsteady ladder. Whatever it was, everything changed that day.

Kevin's expertise and his beautiful wife's talent for singing and helping people, made for a great experience each time I would use their facility. Giving helpful hints, and explaining useful information to make a project better, was one of his gifts. He even offered to play his guitar on one of my songs that we were recording for an album. I am so thankful I knew him.

On a day like so many others, Kevin was taking advantage of not having anyone immediately scheduled to record. As he climbed the ladder to finish some work he was doing, something caused him to fall and strike his head onto the hard wooden floor. He lived a few days before passing away.

I hadn't been to Kevin's studio in quite a while. The cost per hour was prohibitive for me, and I'd discovered a less costly studio right here in Battle Creek. It was during one evening session that the engineer just casually mentioned that another engineer in Kalamazoo had died in an accident. A darkness came over me. He didn't know his name, so after investigating, I confirmed that it was Kevin. The hurt; the emptiness; the fog returned to me. Not exactly the same as when my daughter died, but nonetheless no less shocking and gut wrenching. My friend was gone.

You never get used to Sudden Loss. I've discovered that each time I endure one, those terrible feelings return. I'm so thankful for my perspective and strength during these times which God always provides me with.

They Graced The Sky

The first time I saw them perform was when Ed Sullivan introduced them on his variety show on television one Sunday night in the 1960's. Not far off the stage floor, several members of the Wallenda family walked the wire line. This family was famous throughout the world for their daring high wire act high above the ground without a safety net underneath them.

For years, three members would walk the high wire with their long balancing poles in hand. They would then stop and two others would climb up; one from each side, and place a long pole with a harness hook attached to each end over the shoulders of the three balancing on the wire. Then the two would climb up their shoulders and onto the pole. They would balance there with their own balancing poles sticking out to

36

the sides just like the ones below them. Five incredibly brave individuals defying nature.

Secretly the Wallenda family decided to try the unthinkable. Not many high wire acts had ever had multiple individuals on the high wire at the same time let alone 5 of them. But with a great amount of concentration and guts, they attempted an even more unimaginable task: 7 member's total / 3 levels high. They called it the pyramid. Over and over they would practice. And finally, on national television, they performed it to the delight of a world stage.

But then, after performing the new 7 member act successfully quite a few times, they were at a circus that had packed the huge tent to capacity to see the family live. As always, with no safety net, they began the assembly. The four members on the bottom row got balanced and prepared for the second tier.

When those two were ready and the new pole in place, the last member of this daring act climbed up onto the pole that was balancing on the shoulders of the second tier members. He made it up and balanced himself, to the wild cheers of the crowd far below. But then,- suddenly....

Something went terribly wrong. One or two of the members began to lose their balance, and without warning, four of them came tumbling down to the dirt floor 60 feet below. Two perished and two others were severely injured. Three of the Wallenda's were able to grab hold of the high wire to save themselves. The 3-tier / 7 man pyramid as they called it, was never seen again.

Several of the members of the family continued working in circus's around the world, but always now with a safety net. To watch them perform was always incredible. But danger, and a thing called gravity finally caught up to them.

Reflections

How could these happen I found myself saying. The loss of my cousin on the side of a mountain. A stack of lumber shifts and comes crashing down on a young girl. My good friend falls a short distance and is with us no longer. I will especially miss his musical talent and the encouragement he'd always give to me when I'd go into his recording studio.

A Personal Glimpse of...
Kevin Brown – My Friend & Music Artist

Not many people have crossed my life's path and impacted it like my good friend Kevin Brown. When I first started out in the music business and recording my songs in a professional studio, there always seemed to be something lacking. And then I got the name of the Brown and Brown Recording Studio and found out what professional and personal service and caring were all about.

Located in Kalamazoo, Michigan just southwest of downtown, I first pulled into the driveway of a brick ranch style house in the 1995. Answering the door was an extremely polite and warm welcoming Kevin. Quiet in nature I would soon learn, his vast knowledge and expertise were simply amazing. We talked briefly on the first floor and then went downstairs to his incredible home studio. His massive sound and recording board filled most of one side of the room. Walking through a sliding glass door into the recording room was to me like stepping into a fantasy world; one in which I had only dreamed of in the past.

We did many recordings here over the years together. The most important to me was my daughter Dulcie's memorial album. Through a lot of tears and with the help of a choir of family and friends, we completed the project together. Kevin was masterful at engineering it and so helpful in his suggestions to me on how to make it the best CD possible. We became friends in his sound room with a mutual respect that only artists seem to share.

Years later, Kevin and his wonderful wife Deb bought a downtown building and created a world class studio on the second floor. Taking the old service elevator from decades of servicing a department store was certainly a trip. Entering the sound proof room, I first recorded with a good friend Jonna, and then later with one of Dulcie's best friends in school, Jaime Moore, this studio became my recording home. Kevin was just plain inspirational and marvelous. His knowledge impeccable. And his humor delightful.

I will forever miss Kevin undeniably. His studio picture remains in my office as a reminder of very special times with a caring friend.

HEART ATTACK – RELATIVE/FRIEND

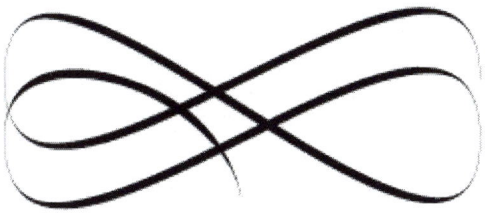

My Grandfather - My Mentor

I was at work at the VA Hospital in Battle Creek, on a sunny and warm spring day in April. It was a little after 2 pm when the call came into the warehouse office. The clerk called for me, and when I picked up the phone, I recognized my mother's quivering voice on the other end. She had some bad news to tell me.

Grandpa Cripps was a great man in my eyes. He was the one who taught me so many of the things that a father would normally teach, because my own dad was always away at work or doing other things. He never had much time for me. Grandpa loved baseball, and once was invited to try out with the Detroit Tigers. He was an electrician by trade and a dedicated family man with four children. We played catch with a baseball often. He would swim, dance, and work hard in the yard every day. I really cared about him.

Mom told me that Grandpa had been outside raking leaves when he grew tired. Entering his house just two doors down from my mom and dad's, he went to the front room overlooking Fine Lake and sat down in his favorite chair that overlooked the water. He asked my grandma to get him a couple of his heart pills because he wasn't feeling very well. When she returned from the kitchen, she found him keeled over in his chair. There was no pulse according to the ambulance crew when they arrived.

I couldn't explain how I felt to my supervisor; only that I had just lost my grandfather. He asked me if I needed to go home and I told him no, that I just needed some time to think. So I wandered the grounds near the warehouse for nearly an hour; sitting on the warm grass in a slight breeze. I wrote a song for him soon after his passing. Like my feelings when I first got the news from Mom, the song's title – "In The Middle Of Nowhere".

My grandfather was a splendid example of a good man who left a special impression on all those around him. He made us laugh and enjoy life; whether at Fine Lake during family get-togethers or at homecoming time in Athens in July.

43

A Special Mother - One Of A Kind

It was late afternoon when my dad called me. I had been busy all day with projects and errands to run. Burl Converse was not an outward show-emotion kind of man. But on this occasion, in his broken voice, you could almost hear the tears streaming down his weathered face. "Your mother is gone, Jerry. I can't believe she's gone"! I told Sally what happened and immediately I headed up to the hospital.

My mother was a classic 1950's mom with a lively twist. Raising us four kids on her own; two boys and two girls, it wasn't easy. But with the support of Grandpa and Grandma Cripps who lived right behind us, she provided everything we needed – especially her unconditional love. She played sports at Athens H.S. when it wasn't fashionable for girls to in the 1940's. Working in the shipyards in Washington State during World War II, she met my father. Years later, she remarried – to her high school sweetheart Burl – my stepfather legally – my Dad in reality. She was liked by everyone and he and her cherished their home at Fine Lake.

When I arrived at the hospital, I found other family members consoling Dad. He gave me a hug with tears in his eyes. Then I walked over to the bed where Mom lay motionless. Having just come to the hospital for a simple test, she told Dad to let the nurse know that she felt nauseous; could she please have something for it. Sitting on the edge of the bed, with Dad next to her, she suddenly and without warning, bent forward and sighed; her last breath in this world.

I loved my mother dearly. So many memories. Such closeness. She worried about me each day I was on duty as a firefighter. She always attended my sporting events when I was in school, and all the other school activities too. She saved me from the attic hornets, and soothed my sun burned body from a day on the beach. Mom was always there for us kids; loved the grandchildren, and adored her husband and friends. She was truly one-of-a-kind.

He Lived Well To The End

In high school, he and I weren't real close, but shared a best friend in Roger. Jim was a friendly guy with kind of a goofy personality. He was an average student. He'd had a heart condition for many years, and was unable to participate in many activities because of it. After graduation, he worked several jobs before joining the transportation department for the city of Battle Creek. He later became the transit supervisor.

I remember how much he loved his wife, and did a fine job for the City. Holiday times, he'd always order my wife Sally's "haystacks" (chocolate covered coconut candy). It was time to go home. The day was at an end. He left the parking lot near West Michigan Avenue and had traveled only a few short blocks, when his worst fear enveloped him.

Jim had joined us on our senior trip, and enjoyed time playing cribbage and chess with Roger and I. He loved the water, and he too lived at Fine Lake where both Roger and I grew up. His dad and I worked at times on the same shift at the fire department. Jim was a good supervisor whom bus drivers and other employees respected and enjoyed being around.

We got the call at #5 firehouse around 6 pm. It came in as a medical / man down. Each day, most of the fire stations around the city would run on medicals, so this was nothing out of the ordinary – or so I thought. We arrived within' three minutes to find a man lying face down in the middle of the intersection; his car was also in the intersection with the driver's door wide open. I immediately began CPR and continued it after the ambulance crew arrived. After a very long time of compressions and breathing, we got a pulse. We loaded him onto a gurney and then into the ambulance. That's when I asked my lieutenant the man's name. It was Jim. I was stunned. I had just revived a friend of mine!

Jim lived for about four days after he had collapsed. Successful CPR had given his family time to spend with him still alive. At the funeral, his wife gave me the biggest hug and asked if I'd please be a last minute poll bearer. It was my privilege.

We never know when Sudden Loss will strike. We also never know when we'll be called upon to do the extraordinary; maybe even to someone very close to our heart.

To Serve Right To The End

He had a knack for making you smile. A good family man with wonderful principles. Ken was the pastor of our church when we lived in Marshall, Michigan. I always loved his messages and the efforts he put into them because he always worked so hard to present it well.

He struggled with his weight. So he began walking. Everywhere! More than once I saw him walking for miles to get to his destination. He started looking much more fit. He dearly loved his family and church family; and a God that helped him serve his small congregation with integrity.

Ken dreamed of writing a book. So he began working on it. It became a passion for him and he diligently put many, many hours into the project. He wrote the very last words down one evening, and then suddenly......he crashed to the floor. He had taken his last breath. With family right there, he was faithful to his cause, and to his God, right up until the end. It hit me pretty hard. I miss him. He was truly a good man.

Reflections

I walked outside of my workplace in shock after hearing the terrible news on the phone from my mother. Grandpa was so active and healthy. My mom was not as healthy. But to hear from my weeping father who never cried made my loss even more difficult. I did CPR on my friend and brought him back to life for a few precious days. These were hard times.

A Personal Glimpse of...

Virginia Converse – My Mother

My mother was an amazing woman. Almost everyone liked being around her because of her bubbly personality, quick wit and big smile. She and my step dad lived at Fine Lake near Battle Creek, Michigan for well over 50 years. They both loved lake living and the many, many friends they had made during their time living there.

Mom raised us four kids alone with the help of my grandparents, Forrest and Gladys Cripps. We all lived on Golden Avenue until 1959 when

Grandpa told my mom about an opportunity to move out to Fine Lake. So on a whim, Grandpa packed up his little trailer house and mom and my step dad packed up the big two room tent, and off we did go.

After they were married, my mom helped my new dad with starting up his own construction business. She was able to stay home and as always, be there for us kids. For all of our school careers from Kindergarten on, she was active as a parent in everything we did.

Mom played basketball in high school when girls in sports were pretty much shunned by the public. She was also a cheerleader and a good student.

She dated her high school sweetheart through her senior year, (my step dad), and after graduation, left him behind so that her and my aunt could go out to Washington State to work in the shipyards during World War II.

She met my father there and they were married, moving to Michigan to begin life after the war. He being a pipe coverer along roadways, was gone much of the time on out of state projects. So mom went about her business of providing for and loving us kids to the very best of her ability.

We learned to play cards and board games during bad weather and she watched over us while we played outside on the sunny days. Mom and her siblings had at one time swum across Fine Lake. Later in life I finally accomplished the same feat as my mother.

Being close to family was very important to my mother. We had many wonderful family gatherings at the lake. What a wonderful growing up time we had with a great mom who always did her best. She will always be loved, fondly remembered and missed.

A Personal Glimpse of...

Forrest Cripps – My Grandfather

My grandfather was a grand man and father figure. He taught me many of the life skills I took with me as my own father was mostly away. Such things as vehicle maintenance and learning to tie a tie. A sense of responsibility he instilled in me was so important. And his love of baseball and the Detroit Tigers will always be his claim to fame. He would often come to me and ask to "have a catch with him".

Forrest had been a really good athlete and back in the 1920's, they played baseball year round. Back then, indoor play at the Battle Creek Central Field House took center stage using an oversized softball they call "Jingles". He and a good friend were both supposed to travel to Detroit for a tryout, but my grandfather met Gladys Smith and they soon married. His chance to play on the big stage was gone. But his love of the game never wavered.

He worked as an electrician his whole life. Leaving school in the eighth grade, he was hired to work on the Mio dam project and later became the head electrician and Percy Jones hospital in Battle Creek, Michigan. Later it became the military's Federal Center where he worked for over 40 years until retiring in 1965 at age 67.

My grandma and he loved living at Fine Lake. He would fish, ice skate and swim during the different seasons even up into his 70's. He loved to dance and would stay out on the dance floor for hours. He loved calling square dances and he and my grandma would also travel the fair circuits with their handmade crafts. He was my inspiration during my growing up years.

One bad habit was his stinky ol' King Edwards cigars. He would light one up in the morning, but after it went out, he would just chew on it the rest of the day.

The holidays were his favorite times spent with all the family. We'd gather at their lake home and celebrate each other with excitement and joy. He was my hero and special mentor. I will forever remember him fondly.

HEART ATTACK – FIRE DEPARTMENT FRIENDS

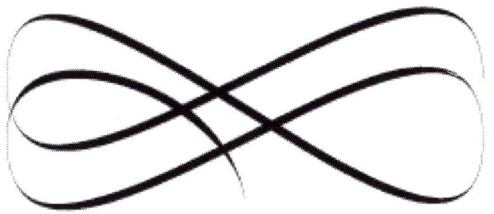

A Last Visit That Almost Wasn't

I had worked with Dan many times on fire and medical calls. He was a confident and competent firefighter who in his spare time, was a leather craftsman and musician. I went to see him and his band play and had him make a belt for my son. He even colored the two little frogs that were engraved on the back. He was in good health as far as anyone knew; a little overweight, but what firefighter wasn't – the casualty of 24 hour shifts.

We received a fire alarm to a garage that was totally involved. It didn't take long to put it out, and during mop up operations, Dan grabbed his chest and had a shortness of breath. An ambulance on the scene, took him immediately to the hospital after taking his vitals. We were later told he had suffered a mild heart attack and that he would be under observation for a few days in the hospital. It was a Friday night when we got the news.

I left church and had some errands to run. I hadn't heard anything new about Dan's condition, and as I approached the hospital, I thought that maybe I would stop in to see him. Then I passed by the entrance because I figured that Dan's family would probably be visiting him on a weekend and so I didn't want to be a bother.

A couple of blocks past the hospital, I told myself to stop procrastinating and turn around. We must prioritize what things are most important in life. And people are the most important of all. So I turned the truck around and returned to the hospital.

As I entered Dan's hospital room, his family was indeed there. He was sitting up and talking. He saw me and was happy I had come. We talked for a short time and informed me he might be back to work this week. He told me he might be going home the next day and thanked me for coming. Feeling so much better having taken the time to visit, I thought to myself, I mustn't put such important things off.

On Monday, Dan passed away from having a massive heart attack.

Agony Of A Firefighter

Harry was a nice guy. Born out east in New York, his heavy accent always gave him away in a crowd. Usually very happy, he had a difficult time grasping a lot of the fire department principles that he needed to be a successful firefighter. Joining the department at an older age, in his 40's, he worked hard at getting better at the job. He always talked of having the same thing back in New York when you discussed having something here in Michigan.

It was a spring morning and there seemed to be more activity than usual at the #1 Fire Station. While having coffee in the eating area, I suddenly heard a lot of commotion on the apparatus floor. Going out to see what was happening, I found Harry yelling at someone in the office.

He was extremely visibly upset. When I tried to console him as he was leaving to go home after his shift, he thanked me for my support and assured me that he would be alright. He left very angry. I was quite concerned about him.

Upon arriving for my next duty day, I received the news. Harry had gone home that morning and began explaining to his wife about what had happened at the station. It might have been over benefits he felt he deserved. He then went into another room to be alone. His wife, concerned after he didn't come out after a long absence, found him on the floor not breathing. Later it was determined he had had a massive heart attack.

Calm Before The Chaos

He seemed always in good spirits. I had many chances to work with him and always enjoyed the job together and after work time. He was witty and fun to be around.

Vacation time was something he enjoyed a lot. And being in a boat fishing was about as good as it got for him. With seemingly nothing wrong physically, we received the news that Emil had died of a heart attack while on that vacation. It saddened me that another of my firefighting comrades had passed away. I knew I would miss him. I'm glad I got to know him.

Reflections

As a firefighter, we are a very close knit group. To lose someone you work with is difficult enough. To have a close friendship with them makes it even harder. For two of them, I heard about it upon returning to work for my next shift. I am so glad I took the time to visit the third in the hospital while he was recuperating. I'm so grateful that I went to see him once more before he unexpectedly passed away.

In Its Quickness

By Jerry H. Ball

In its quickness, the life is gone! But not what, in goodness, which that life pursued. Each person has given so much to some or the many. And all of us have shared love; a lot or a little. How was our life while we lived it, might be a question to ask ourselves.

Those who grieve will remember us, and what we did; depending on all that it was for them. We have but one earthly life. How we've spent it, will be the memories of those whose lives we've touched.

So it is wise and good that we should try our best to use our God given gifts, and maybe, just maybe, we'll enrich the lives of many of those who are around us. And then, almost assuredly, they will remember us in a very special way.

It is not for us to pursue just doing good deeds and looking for reward. But it is in those deeds done, that we will leave our imprint. May each of us strive to perfect our being humble, loyal, caring, hardworking, dedicated, friendly, courteous, searching for truth, and living a life that is pleasing to God and all of those around us while we're here.

May we each be a blessing to people everywhere. May our legacy be filled with good and well-meaning things. And may our regrets be printed onto a very short list, as we work diligently to live life to the very best of our ability.

HOMICIDE – RELATIVE/ASSOCIATE

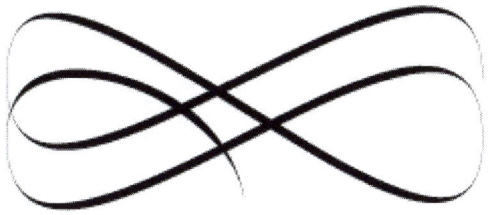

So Strong And Brave

He was a very large man who had his share of disappointments and trials in his life. At age 13, he was playing in a barn when suddenly he slipped and fell onto the solid wooden floor far below, breaking his arm. Rushing him to the doctor, who was in a hurry to go on vacation, Mel's arm was set improperly. Gangrene set in.

In the 1930's, the protocol was to amputate just above where the gangrene was. There was a fight to save the rest of his arm as gangrene kept returning. Now almost up to his shoulder, the doctor's told his parents that there was nothing more they could do should this last surgery not stop it. The gangrene did not return.

In 1975, having retired from their small business, Mel and Geri had purchased a motor home so they could travel comfortably around the country; and especially to their daughter's home in Reno, Nevada.

Major plans were made, and finally came the day to leave their Michigan home on the St. Joe river, and head west.

Mel didn't like young men with long hair; they were "hippies" to him.

When he first met me, his future son in law, I had long hair. So when they were crossing the great plains of Oklahoma and came across a hitch hiker who was clean cut, he didn't see any reason not to pick him up. He was a polite young man. But this young man had a very dark secret.

After a long day of traveling, the couple bedded down for the night. The young man was in the bedroom at the opposite end of the motor home. Hearing noises, Mel got up to find the visitor seemingly high on something.

Going from quiet and reserved, the man had found a butcher knife and demanded Mel and Geri lie down on the floor, where he first tied her up, and then prepared to tie him up as well. But before he could finish his evil plan, Mel turned on him and wrestled the man to the floor. The

61

knife still in the young man's hand, made its first serious incision into Mel's body, and then a second and third, and…. The continuous stabbings soon began to take their toll.

Realizing that the young man's intent was to kill them both, Mel screamed at Geri to somehow get out of the motor home. She wiggled her way to the door and with difficulty, got it open. While her husband continued to wrestle with the assailant, she managed to crawl onto the pavement at the truck stop where they had stopped for the night.

Screaming for help, the locals converged on the motor home, where they found Mel lying motionless on the floor from 19 stab wounds; the assailant – soon would be captured! Geri would return back to Michigan; so very different from when they had left not that long ago.

My wife and I received the horrible news around 11:15 p.m.; the telephone in the bedroom startling us awake. As I sat on the edge of the bed listening to my brother in law describe the tragedy, I quickly relayed the information to my wife who already knew something was terribly wrong.

An assessment; bad judgment; one unspeakable night in Oklahoma. How quickly things can change in one's life. How quickly can one's life change.

A Beautiful Child - So Short A Time

While in the U.S. Army, finishing up my three year tour from August to December 3rd, my wife, toddler son and I arrived in Killeen, Texas. The little town bordered Fort Hood and wasn't too far from Dallas. My wife loved buying Avon products and soon got the name of a dealer living near town.

The woman who answered the front door, was young and very nice. She welcomed us in, and we took a seat on the couch while she went to get our order. In a playpen in one corner of the living room, was a beautiful little long haired four year old girl. She seemed happy and smiled at us as we said hello. When our business was finished, we shared pleasantries and then told the mother that we looked forward to seeing her again.

I worked in the office for our unit in Fort Hood as a company clerk, so I was sort of a receptionist for all the soldiers who would come in to see the Captain. I remember so well, the day the young private entered and was so excited that he was finally getting the back pay for his wife. It was quite a substantial sum of money. He walked out with the paperwork he would need at the finance office, and had a big smile on his face. But to me, something seemed out of sorts. I just didn't know what.

It was a week or so when I received the terrible news. That beautiful little four year old girl was found under water in the bathtub by police who had received a 911 call from the father. The police became suspicious almost immediately as the father showed little emotion, and the little girl had multiple marks on her body. Further investigation showed major head trauma.

When no one could account for the whereabouts of the mother for several weeks, the pieces began to fall into place for the authorities. With the mother evidently skipping across state lines with the large sum of money, the father was soon arrested and charged in the little girl's death.

Innocence Brought The End

What brings a man to do unspeakable things to another? Always lurking in the shadows are those who just don't care. On a dark night around 12 am., he stood outside the glass door waiting.

Nichole was a good person. Sometimes she ended up befriending someone a little unsavory and her friends would let her know. Someone she'd recently met, decided at closing time to pay her a visit at the convenience store where she worked. Just five minutes before, a young man, a friend of ours who frequented the business, got his gas; talked with her briefly, and then left.

It seems she unlocked the door for him. It was just past closing time. He proceeded to rob the store and then attacked her. Without conscious, he brutally ended her life. Within' hours, after she was discovered, police   arrested the man who had no feelings at all on the matter.

Several hundred people stood outside the store in a vigil for their fallen friend. She absolutely didn't deserve this end. No one does!

One Little Boy And His Monster

He never smiled a lot whenever I was around him. But the little 4 year old seemed happy enough. A good friend of my family, Ben, had started dating his mother, and there seemed to be harmony in the relationship.

Ben loved the little boy and treated him like he was his own son. They lived in a quiet neighborhood where calm seemed to be the norm. But something didn't seem right to me about the mother, yet I couldn't put my finger on it. She seemed very distant from her own child – almost like he was a bother in her life. When they came to our church some Sundays, Ben was always the one who would pick him up from Sunday school.

The mother worked late one night. Ben was caring for the boy and had put him to bed in his room at the normal time. He tucked him in and kissed him goodnight. Several hours later, his mother came home. After getting ready for bed, she went in to check on her son and returned to bed saying he took a deep breath, sighed and then rolled over.

The next morning, a horror beyond any parent's worst nightmare. The boy wasn't breathing. His lifeless little body lay motionless on his bed. In total disbelief, Ben could not stop sobbing. 911 was called. When the ambulance arrived, the crew took vitals and declared that he had no heartbeat or signs of life. The mother's reaction seemed almost put on. Not much emotion.

The following 12 months were excruciating as Ben was charged with murder but later exonerated from the charges. He spent over nine months of his life in jail for a crime he did not commit. And the mother? She will be judged someday, that's for certain.

Reflections

Tragedy doesn't begin to describe your feelings when you hear the news that someone has viciously and without conscious, taken the life of another human being. It always seems so senseless. Not one of these deserved to die so young. Not expecting a late night call. Not expecting to not be able to fall back to sleep. Not expecting to................

A Personal Glimpse of...

Melvin Rooker – My Father-In-Law

My father in law was a large man who grew up under mostly normal circumstances. As a thirteen year old, a good playground was the barn. On one unforgettable day however, his life would be changed forever.

While with a playmate, Mel unfortunately fell from the loft area and ultimately broke his arm. In severe pain, his mother rushed him to see his doctor who was preparing at that moment to leave on vacation. In a hurry to leave, the doctor set his arm incorrectly. The complications and effects of that mistake would cost the young man dearly.

Mel had to return to the hospital several times over the passing months because gangrene had set in and back in those days, amputation was the prescribed resolution. First taking off his lower arm and then just above the elbow, when the gangrene returned a third time, the family was told that this was the last time they could do surgery; that if it returned there was nothing more that could be done. It must have been an extremely frightening time. The gangrene did not return. He would now have to learn how to live with one arm.

The first time we met was in early 1968. He thought I was a "hippy" with my long hair and a beard. It bothered him that his little girl was dating this freaky character. Over time however, we learned to get along. With my helping him with several projects around his house, our relationship grew more positive and stronger – the young man who would eventually marry his one and only daughter.

He worked for a friend who owned an ice cream delivery company who supplied business's with product. After surgery, Mel needed time to recuperate, but the owner refused him time off and they soon parted ways. Out of work and not knowing what to do, he and my mother in law Geri built and then operated their own successful business until they both retired and planned on doing a lot of traveling.

Mel was a very gruff individual on the exterior, but the love he had for his wife and daughter was always strong. He will always be remembered as a man who would not let adversity keep him down.

HOMICIDE – FIRE DEPARTMENT RUN

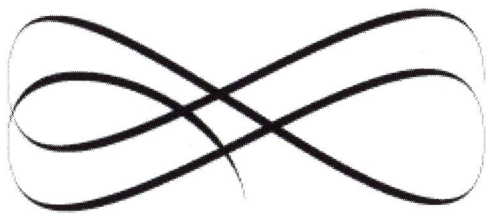

A Sinister Plan Unthinkable Acts

Several human beings act out unspeakable atrocities on four unsuspecting women. What started out as a robbery plan, ended in the death of two innocent women in a local massage parlor and the permanent unstable and the cruelest of emotional scars I have ever witnessed.

As a member of the fire department, I had seen many unnerving things. And even though I wasn't on duty this horrible night, I was totally in disbelief of what I was told. Never had I heard a real life story of such cruelty and disregard for human dignity and life, ever. And in my home town.

Three men and a woman stopped at the front of the parlor with the intent to rob. Two of the men entered through the front door; the leader of the group and one of his followers. The woman remained behind the wheel of the car.

After being given money by the attendants, the two men began beating the women relentlessly and into submission. The victims were then cut and caustic liquid was poured on them, as well as other heinous acts of cruelty.

Two of the women finally escaped the building screaming for their lives. The other two women eventually perished from their injuries.

Years later, following one of the most tragic events that the fire department had ever run on, I was on duty and we received a call for a medical emergency located in one of the most exclusive areas of town.

Arriving on the scene, screams could be heard coming from inside the house. Approaching with caution, a man appears inside an open front door. He is visibly distraught and yet fairly calm in his actions. Upon entering the home, a woman can be seen on the staircase leading to the upstairs. She's just lying there on the carpeted stairs; seemingly out of breath. The ambulance crew arrives.

71

The husband of the woman describes how out of the clear blue, his wife would begin screaming and flailing her arms as if fighting off someone. He's attempted to get her psychological help in a variety of forms, but nothing has helped. He then explained that she was one of the two women who had been tortured at the massage parlor but had escaped. He said he could no longer take it – the way she was.

For this woman, the nightmares and the emotional breakdown that was now her life, would probably never end. A human being is extremely resilient. And yet one can only endure so much pain, suffering and torture, before the person's emotional stability is shattered and the results are permanent.

One Knock One Horrible Ending

Police and the fire department work hand in hand on many crime scenes as well as on other runs. We got to know many of the police officer's well and some by name. It was a great relationship.

With Officer Braun, you always knew you could trust his judgment; that he would never put you in harm's way. It was a sunny day when he and another officer went to the apartment complex to talk to a possible suspect. A quick knock at the door and then wait.

As the door opened, a woman stood in the doorway and when asked about the suspect, he quickly showed up behind her holding a gun. He then pointed it directly at the officer and fired. No remorse; not an ounce of conscious. In an instant, one of the finest officers in the Battle Creek Police Department was gone.

The suspect that was being sought for questioning and who exacted a terrible toll on all of us, said he was just trying to scare the officer. But the truth was clear. We continue to miss Officer Braun. He was truly a credit to his very dangerous profession.

So Unexpected So Quick

The ideal family. A husband and wife both taught for the Battle Creek Public Schools. Their children attended there of course and were good students. People everywhere were always commenting on how well behaved the kids were. But that was out in public. What went on behind closed doors? One afternoon, after school, both mom and dad arrived back home at the usual time.

Whether something awful had just happened or a long list of things had disturbed one of their son's, he decided to change the way things were. When the car pulled into the garage and the door automatically closed, the couple opened their doors and got out. That's when the young man came into view with a gun in his hand. It only took a moment. So unexpected; so quick.

Why would a young teenage boy be so desperate and so depressed that he would want to harm his parents? This question may never be answered.

Reflections

Why? Innocent people should not be subjected to "one minute everything's normal," and then it happens. The four young women working late one night, could never have suspected the incredibly diabolical mind of a deranged man entering and then with others, torturing them. And the two survivors will never be emotionally the same ever, ever again.

"Grief is a journey that can either have a good ending
or no ending."
-        Bethany Blankinship

HOMICIDE – PUBLIC

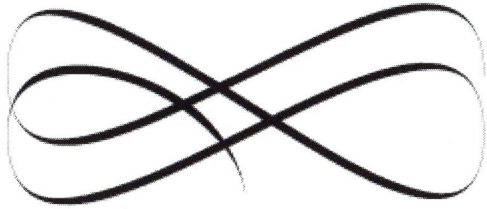

Inconvenience Easy Enough To Remedy

There have been some events that have occurred in my lifetime that will always haunt me. So many times they have to do with children. Mine are the most important people in my life because they always seem to somehow need their dad. And their age doesn't matter. One particular incident stands out and is probably more heinous than almost any other to me.

A young woman in her late 20's had two children. She was the perfect mother to those who knew her. They were well dressed; well cared for. But she had a dark secret and the children were not part of her future plans. She placed the two kids in their car seats in the back seat of her car, strapped them in, and then drove to a remote lake.

She was frantic. Her two children were suddenly missing; someone took them! They'd just vanished. Quickly, search parties were organized and law enforcement went into action. A massive hunt was under way. For more than a week, news reporters interviewed the mother; her agony; her loss. It was front page news every day. And then, suddenly, there was a break in the case. But it was not what anyone would ever have expected.

In that same remote lake, a car was spotted; submerged under the water. A wrecker was brought in and it slowly pulled the vehicle from the watery depths. Spectators and reporters anxiously watched. There was something inside. The car was identified. It was the young woman's car. And still strapped in their car seats, were two precious children.

I'm so saddened by what this woman did. She meticulously planned and cunningly deceived a nation – for just a little while. Maybe terrible things happen so the rest of us can learn something from it. Or maybe it's so we can look into the dark side of a human being; so the evil deed won't be repeated.

And maybe it's to remind us to give that extra hug at night, or a goodbye kiss to our little ones before heading off to work each day. Or maybe it's to let us know that we should make every effort to be kinder to one another. Because we never know when Sudden Loss will show itself once more.

The First Day Lasting Forever

She had just graduated from Delton Kellogg High School and had started her very first day on the job at the local bank across from the supermarket. It was so exciting for her to begin her first job and a promising career. She was a pretty girl and extremely personable. Everyone at the bank looked forward to working with her.

Several young men entered the bank without any fanfare. After a few minutes of talking to the new bank teller, they took out guns and demanded money. As the young girl reached down to get the money out of her drawer, an extremely nervous and fidgety robber thought he saw her reach for the alarm button. Without hesitation, he raised his rifle, and pointing it at her, pulled the trigger.

Apprehended a short time later, the young men were whisked away to a waiting jail cell. In the briefest of moments, a beautiful young woman was violently taken away from us in the least likely of small towns. A great sadness overtook the townspeople. They remembered a very special young woman who had barely begun her life's journey. What began as a day of promise, ended in awful tragedy.

How Could You Do It

Sometimes we just can't understand how someone could perform such a heinous act. How could anyone be so depressed and/or angry to lead them to harming a child. But what do we really know about other people anyway.

It was Christmas Eve morning and the father of two young boys decided he wanted to show them where he worked. The factory made metal products and the man worked in an area where there was a blast furnace. The car pulled into the now vacant parking lot and the three got out. The man knew how to get in.

As the two youngsters looked around, the disturbed man pondered his life. Many things had gone terribly wrong including his marriage. So he had decided that this was what he was going to do. Only he walked back out the door of the factory that morning. What he'd just done was unspeakable. He drove away alone. The image of this story is still horribly disturbing.

Of So Much Hatred

I always hated bullying. I received my share of it when I was in school and at times, it was devastating! But mostly I just sucked up the emotion and moved on. Still it was hard each day; the thought that one of the bullies at school might be lurking; waiting to strike. Those days were basically harmless. What I read in the paper one day, was not.

Also on the evening news, a young man in Texas lived a different lifestyle than those around him. So much prejudice, and yet he never struck back. He was kind and thoughtful, and would never harm anyone. But that's not how everyone living in the little town was.

Out for a joyride in a pickup truck on a gravel country road, three young men in their late 20s, saw the young man walking just ahead of them. Hateful of those who they said, "just didn't fit in", they at first pulled alongside of him just to be verbally abusive. When they didn't get the response they were looking for, they got mad and stopped the truck.

Two of the men grabbed the young man and held him until the third man grabbed a long piece of rope and tied it around his feet. The other end was tied to the bumper of the truck. Then the three men got back into the truck and the driver gave it some gas, knocking the young

81

man down. Then they mercilessly and hideously drove down the road about ten miles an hour to the screams coming from behind. Not too long after this horrendous act began, there was silence - it was over.

They stopped and untied the rope from the truck, and drove off laughing. There was no regard for the welfare of the critically injured young man, who would soon die from his injuries. This unspeakable act happens more often than people want to admit. Prejudice and hatred have no place in any society. Justice for these three men must be served.

Reflections

A few things make me cringe. Extreme sadness for a young girl's family. Incredulously that three men would incapacitate someone and then drag him. A totally distraught father who loves his children, horrifically ends their young lives. And the most disturbing, a mothers total disregard for human life and the unbelievable torture of her own precious children.

MEDICAL – FIRE DEPARTMENT RUN

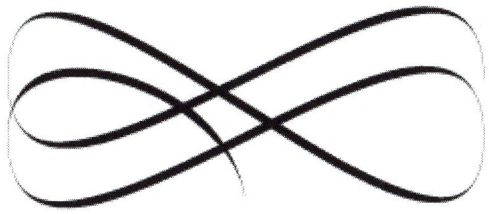

The Unbelievably Unbearable Truth

I was working on the fire department that morning; the station in Battle Creek located near the I-94 freeway. We got the medical call around 11 a.m. As we were en route, the dispatcher described the victim as a small child not breathing. With the adrenaline now pumping at an accelerated rate, we race to the location only a few blocks away.

It was a clear day with the sun shining through the tall trees. Stopping in front of the tri-level home, we hurry inside to find a woman, the day care provider for several children including Hunter and his sister, doing CPR on a small child. She had dialed 911 and then had a neighbor call Hunter's mother to tell her that she needed to return to the child care center as soon as possible. What could be so important? What has happened to one of my children?

As I take over and do CPR on the small little boy, the ambulance crew arrives along with a police officer. A short time later, a vehicle screeches to a halt in the street in front of the house. The mother frantically runs towards the house when the neighbors and the police officer stop her.

We stop and take vitals one more time, and that's when the ambulance crew declares an end to our efforts. The child has passed away. That's also when she is told outside of the house, the unbelievable news about her little boy.

I have never heard such a heart wrenching and blood curdling scream of pain as on that horrible morning. I'm now holding the child while sitting on the floor. The sobbing mother is finally allowed to enter the house and incredulously looks down on a firefighter holding the lifeless body of her beloved son.

She asks if she can hold him. I gently place him in her arms as she sits down in a rocking chair. The look on her face is so similar to the one I had on a Thanksgiving afternoon not so long ago

I wrote a loving poem for little Hunter and gave it to his mom and dad at the funeral home. Days later, they asked if my wife and I might come over to their home for a visit. The grieving parents thanked me for all I'd done that afternoon for their son. And thanked me also for the poem which was now framed and placed in a position of honor on the wall. It was a very touching time for all of us. A short time later, we left that home with heartfelt memories of one very special little three year old boy.

It was discovered after his death, that he had had a heart defect since birth.

A Little Boy Gone Too Quickly

Will, as always, went to work that morning for the ambulance service without any reservations to what the day might hold in store. He loved his job; helping people and saving lives. He grew close to many of the firefighters, like me, because of the working relationship between the two emergency service providers and the city and surrounding area protocols. On any emergency call, you would nearly always see an ambulance and a fire rig on the scene; especially in the city of Battle Creek.

As he prepared to leave early this morning, he gave his wife a kiss and then his sleeping son. Pausing for a moment, he looked down at the little boy peacefully lying there. His family was such a blessing to him and he was so thankful each day for all he was given.

Not too long into his shift, a call came in. Somehow, the residential address seemed way too familiar. It suddenly hit Will that "this particular call" was his house! Expeditiously the vehicle sped away with lights and siren going. Unbeknownst to him and his wife, their little boy had a heart defect at birth. From what seemed an uneventful beginning to the day to him, now suddenly brought extreme anxiety and uncertainty. With his heart pounding, the rig pulled into his driveway.

A friend explains to me about what's happened to his co-worker and friend. In tears, he's not sure how to handle it. We talk a long time and I console him as best I can. I cannot imagine what Will and his wife are now going through. My daughter was 19. His son, just 3. So little time with such a precious child.

A Baby Remembered The First Call

I had only been on the fire department a short time when my first trouble breathing call came in. Sitting in the living room area at the station, the Claxton alarm (very loud) went off. It would send your heart racing as you headed quickly for the rig (fire engine). I got my rubber goods on and boarded the engine to head towards Green Street.

En route, the dispatcher repeated the original message, "Trouble breathing; infant". Now our hearts were really racing. We arrived on the scene in less than 3 minutes and quickly went inside.

The small child, 6 months old, was turning a grayish-blue and unresponsive. There were two of us doing CPR on the little boy. The lieutenant, who was overseeing our efforts to revive him, kept whispering, "Come on little baby, come on baby, breath"!!! The ambulance showed up and stood by as we continued working on the child.

It seemed like an eternity. We tried so hard and wanted so badly to suddenly hear the sound of air and gasping by the little boy, but it never came. As the ambulance crew finally whisked him away, we departed the scene quietly and sadly.

I knew when I took the test for the firefighter position, that it would be a great job. Helping people; saving lives; adrenaline pumping; excitement! What I didn't expect or could have known, was the stark reality of this same job. I wasn't prepared for what I'd just experienced –

not being able to bring someone back to life. How would I handle this? I called my wife and sadly told her about the experience.

Through my career I would go on many runs like this and perform CPR on countless individuals. I mentally and emotionally survived my first time. It was very difficult, and yet I knew we did everything possible on that day we pulled up on Green Street in an attempt to rescue one little baby.

Reflections

Eerie and haunting is how it feels when such young children die in your arms. Super sadness comes over you when you realize there's nothing more you can do. I will never forget my lieutenant on the fire department whispering, "Breathe baby," And the echoing, excruciating guttural scream of a young mother who has suddenly lost her loving little boy.

A Personal Glimpse of...
Ken Tippin – My Pastor and Friend

There are men of God who definitely live their faith on their sleeve if you will. Ken Tippin did that and more. He was a professor of faith who always put his heart and soul into his sermons for all in attendance to witness and enjoy. Such a Godly man was he.

Ken loved his wife Betty Ruth and his children more than anything other than God himself. I met him for the first time at the Church of God on Cosmopolitan Street in Marshall, Michigan for a Sunday morning service. When I moved to Marshall, I wanted to attend the same denomination church as I did in Battle Creek, so this little church fit the bill for me.

Warmly greeted by the small congregation, I quickly grew to appreciate the spirit of the families attending and by a pastor with a fervor for teaching the words of Jesus to his people. The messages always had a profound message and many times I walked out the doors feeling inspired by the words of this pastor.

In 1990, I was remarried in this little church with Ken Tippin officiating. It was a glorious time of uniting two people who had first met within' it's walls just a year before during a Sunday morning service. It felt so right being blessed by Ken's words of encouragement during the very special ceremony.

Pastor Ken had always struggled with food and its profound impact on his weight problem. Many times he had tried dieting but soon after beginning, things would cause him to fall back into old patterns. But then his will power and determination to finally succeed in losing weight took hold and he began a whole new journey in his life.

While writing a book that he had long wanted to complete, he began walking and watching his diet. He made a serious effort to avoid past mistakes and temptations. And he'd walk. And walk everywhere in his quaint little town. The weight began coming off in droves. He knew he was on the path to better health and hopefully a longer life. I was so proud of his efforts and we continued to grow as friends throughout the remaining years of his life. A very special man who was so blessed by a God well pleased.

MEDICAL – UNEXPLAINABLE

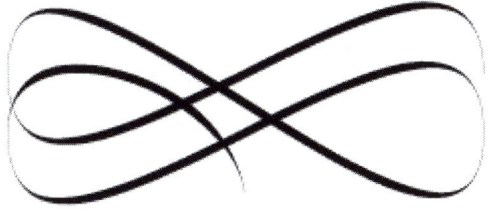

A Tree For Climbing And Crying

Cody was a bright and lively little boy who lived with his family in a suburb of Battle Creek. His house was located across the street from a field where several trees provided for great climbing and having an adventure. He and one of his siblings along with several neighbor children were all playing together when one of the kids ran back to Cody's house and in a panic, told his mother to come quickly.

As the little boy of six climbed one of the trees on this cold winter's day, his partially zipped winter coat got tangled in a branch above him. Trying to free it, Cody slipped off the branch he was standing on and was now dangling from the tree with the coat around his neck. He couldn't breath! The mother frantically attempted to free him; finally getting him to the ground and then to her house where she began rescue breathing.

Fire Department Engine 5 arrived on the scene within' 3 minutes of the alarm and entered the house where we found the little boy's mother on the floor frantically trying to revive him. I relieved her and began CPR.

The ambulance crew arrived, and eventually they attempted to shock him in hopes to get his heart started again. After many attempts, the paramedics announced we would discontinue operations.

It was so difficult for the family! As we left the scene, the tears welled up in my eyes, as I began thinking of my own small children. How sad and empty this family was going to be. How difficult it is to have a day when everything is so happy and the sound of laughing children suddenly and horribly turns to silence.

Arriving back at the fire station, we waited for the defusing team and then discussed the event and emotionally poured out our feelings. It was a very difficult time in both my life and career as a firefighter first responder.

So Wanted - So Difficult - Terrible Grief

Everything seemed perfect for him! The perfect wife, job and now a baby on the way. It just seemed like everything was going right. Dan loved his new job very much. While on duty, he met and fell in love with Sherry, a medic in the ambulance service. Plans were made; family and friends were excited; a wedding and a new house. And not too far in the future, a third person in the home.

Visiting the doctor for her regular monthly visits, everything was going extremely well. Sherry tried her very best to be healthy and provide all the nutrients her baby would need to grow healthy and strong. But then when she went in for her 8 month visit, something wasn't right.

She had noticed at home, that the baby wasn't moving as much, so she voiced her concern to her doctor. Upon checking her, a serious look came over the doctor's face. An ultra sound was taken. The baby wasn't moving. The umbilical cord was wrapped around the baby's neck. There was no heartbeat.

The terrible shock! It Can't Be!! WHY?
NOOOOOOOOOOOO!!!!!!!!!!!!!!

It was a Friday morning when I received a call from Dan. He sounded very serious. He asked me if I could come over to talk about my daughter Dulcie, and how I had coped with her death. I told him absolutely that I would come!

On a hot afternoon, Dan, Sherry and I sat in their living room and began discussing their situation. Everything had been perfect through 32 weeks. And then, just before her last monthly visit, Sherry noticed that something wasn't right. The doctor gave them the horrific news.

Worse still, the doctor said that she would have to wait a few days to see if her body would abort the baby. If not, then the baby would have to be surgically removed. Sherry and Dan not only had to deal with the death of their precious first born to be, she now had to carry it inside her knowing that the little life that should have been, would never be.

They asked me so many questions. How did I immediately deal with Dulcie's death? How old was she? Was it terribly hard each new day to live without her? As the conversation went on, I sensed some uneasy relief from the two of them just being able to talk about their situation with someone else who has had to endure the loss of a child. They thanked me for coming. In the days following my visit, I wrote them a little poem which they greatly appreciated.

It was important for me to attend the funeral. Such a little casket I thought. Both Dan and Sherry remained strong throughout the service. I had the opportunity to meet other family members. It was a very solemn event. I grieved for them quite a long time on my own. I could not imagine what they had just gone through. What courage they showed in the face of the unthinkable. Two remarkable people enduring an impossible situation.

Helpless - A Mother's Cry

The day was so ordinary. No bad weather to drive in and no distractions. The mother pulls her van into the driveway of their home in Ceresco and turns the engine off. That's when she hears a muffled sound coming from the rear of the vehicle.

She can't see her little boy, and suddenly panic sets in. She rushes to the back seat where she finds that her son has slid between the seat itself and the back of the seat. His little body below; his head trapped above; he can hardly breath. She frantically begins screaming for help!

A mechanic nearby hears the mother's screams and rushes to her son's aid. But try as he might, is unable to free the little boy. Again and again he tries to free him but nothing works. He is later pronounced dead at the scene.

The anguish and terror of being helpless for this mother and those who tried to rescue her child, had to be nothing less than excruciating. Having small children and owning a van, it made me think a little more about the safety of my own children while in our vehicle. I think about this Sudden Loss often and each time, sadness once again reveals itself in me.

Reflections

There's a darkness that creeps over you when the unexpected arrives very subtly. How could I console this grieving mother, or say the right words to a couple with such high hopes and love for their first and yet unborn child. And having many children and owning vans, I think sadly and often of this mother who so helplessly watched her son take his last breath.

MEDICAL – QUESTIONS WHY

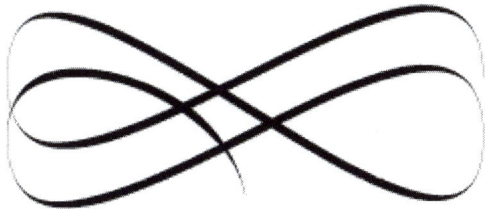

So Innocent - So Many Questions Why

With tiny babies and infants, the parents always have underlying concerns of whether they are okay. We are constantly watching over them. We feed and clothe them; give them baths; burp and then change their diapers; watch them smile and grow and giggle. And yet there's one event that these same parents fear more than any other, and its name is SIDS.

The title was given years ago to babies who are suddenly found lifeless, mostly in their cribs. On the fire department late one morning, we were dispatched to a home where the grandfather couldn't arouse a response from his baby grandson. The baby definitely was gone. Having had five children, when they were babies, I always had that fear in me. I looked down at the tiny little being in the crib; motionless; lifeless. My heart ached. The ambulance crew showed up and relieved us. The image of that little baby will always stay with me. The heartache - always remembered.

It Was Just A Little Something

Jan was my best friend Roger's wife. She was lively and fun to be around. Normally healthy, there was little concern when she went into the hospital for some minor tests. She wasn't feeling good, but there was nothing to worry about. Or was there?

At the time, a lot of people were complaining about the care that was given at this hospital. Some people believed it was a death sentence to go there, so they would travel some distance to another hospital in a different city. Jan didn't see the need to go anywhere else. She trusted her instincts. Everything would be fine.

Thinking that maybe being admitted overnight was a good idea because she started feeling worse, the next day brought concern to both her and Roger. It just didn't seem the hospital was caring for her properly. What should have been simple, became alarming.

On Friday, a lung specialist was supposed to check her, but never showed up. Then over the weekend, her condition worsened. By Monday, she was in a coma and the doctor told Roger to notify the family. Later that day, she passed away.

At the funeral, Roger and I said very little but hugged and comforted each other. It's so difficult when things go terribly wrong when what's supposed to happen, like what didn't in that hospital room, go awry. Questions and ethics came into play. Attorneys were involved. But Jan was gone. And we live on and wonder what could have, and should have been, in our minds.

A Special Time Then Tragedy

Everything was going as planned. The long awaited western trip was truly about to begin. With the Harper Creek family all packed up, they headed down the road and turned onto the westbound ramp of I-94 and a wonderful time of family fun and togetherness. Very close knit, they all had so looked forward to this time together. The teenage daughter was thrilled they were finally under way.

About three days into their journey, the daughter became seriously ill. With a high fever and going delusional, they rushed her to the hospital. After an array of tests, the young girl was diagnosed with spinal meningitis, a mostly fatal disease. For several days the family painfully waited at her bedside. And then she was gone.

A trip so promising ended in the most unbelievable and heart wrenching way. Their beloved little girl, such a vital part of their family, would never shine her beautiful smile again.

Reflections

Questions always arise in your mind when no answers are readily available. A sudden disease. What seemed minor evidently wasn't. And S.I.D.s. I looked down on the tiny infant in his little crib and instantly tears welled up in my eyes. Why God, these little ones? Take good care of them.

MEDICAL – FAMILY/FRIEND

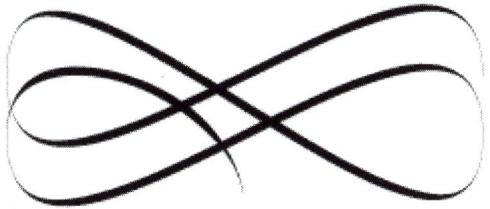

I Never Really Knew Her

My Great Grandma Smith, was always so quiet. When I'd walk across the driveway on Golden Avenue to Grandma Cripps house, she would always be sitting in a rocking chair. She was very old. I only remember her talking to me once, but I was very young and may not have remembered other times. I loved my family and this stately woman was a big part of it.

What I didn't know, is that each of Grandma Smith's kids would take her in for part of the year to live with them for a time. It was a warm spring morning when I stood at the back screen door and watched as Grandma Smith was being helped into my grandpa's car. Nothing unusual about that. My little mind couldn't comprehend, however, that when my grandpa returned, Grandma Smith was not with him. She couldn't return. I never understood why. I never talked about it, but that question haunted me for a very long time. She passed away quietly at my great aunts home.

Older / Younger An Enduring Friendship

My daughter Dulcie, around 12 years old, began a friendship with and elderly woman in our neighborhood in Battle Creek. Often she would ask if she could go and visit her friend just around the corner from where we lived. Her best friend Ann would be waiting, and the two of them would walk together to the senior woman's home on Wentworth Street.

For several years, an enduring relationship made my daughter's life fuller and taught her meaning and great respect being around the elderly. I had the privilege of walking with Dulcie over to this lady's home once. Meeting her was a real pleasure. We talked briefly and then I let the two friends visit alone.

One day my daughter came to me with tears in her eyes. Her elderly friend had suddenly passed away. I consoled and thanked her for the special friendship she had developed with the neighbor. Dulcie asked if I would take her to the funeral. We cried together and spent time remembering a very special woman in my young daughter's life.

A Baby Unborn A Life Stilled

We were young and in love. My wife and I had only been married a short time. I was working two part time jobs to support us. We had an apartment in an old house with two other units. Just the three of us – including our Persian haired cat. Life was good!

Then one day Shirley told me she had missed her period. We didn't have any extra money, and without insurance, I wasn't sure what to do if she was pregnant. I prayed hard that she wasn't. Time went by. No telltale signs of anything.

I worked for BC News who distributed bundles of newspapers to businesses. While out on my route, I received word to call my boss right away. I got to a pay phone and Jerry Brown told me that Shirley was in the hospital; she was doing just fine, but had had a miscarriage. I rushed up to Community Hospital. I suddenly was relieved, but struggled with the loss of a child. Wow! How could one tiny being affect me even when I never got to see him or her. It would leave a profound impact on my feelings for the unborn.

Reflections

When my great grandmother left that day, I had no idea that would be the last time. But being small, it didn't affect me very much since I'd never really gotten to know her. But when I got the news that my wife is in the hospital and nature had taken my unborn child, a storm of emotions came over me. Sometimes there are no answers, just accepting the reality.

A Personal Glimpse of...
Roger Hussong – My Best Friend

A best friend is even better to have that a good one. Roger and I certainly enjoyed our roles as inseparable buddies all through late elementary, high school and two years at Kellogg Community College in Battle Creek, Michigan. Working on science projects, learning to water ski, playing chess, monopoly and always football and baseball games. There were few times you wouldn't find us hanging out together.

Roger and his adopted mom were very close. She would always spend time making a large grocery bag full of popcorn for the three of us at the auto theatre. She was a constant supported for his activities and throughout his life.

Neither of us could wait for the snow to melt so we could play catch with a baseball. Then there were the sandlot baseball and football games with all the neighborhood kids that lasted all day. During our college years, racquetball became our favorite indoor sport while always; golf took center stage during the summer at Maple Hills golf course near Augusta.

Just before high school graduation, Roger and I and our girlfriends spent an incredible day on the beaches of beautiful Lake Michigan. Good clean fun on a beautiful and unforgettable day. For graduation, with both of us being fairly short, we fell to near the end of the line but held our heads high as we proudly received our diplomas from Delton Kellogg High School.

Together we found an apartment together to share expenses. With both of us working at the Eaton Corporation for the summer, we were able to start saving for college in the fall. Roger eventually moved back home to save money. We continued to stay in close contact with one another until he left for Central Michigan University for further studies.

Roger found the love of his life in Jan. They moved into the house where he grew up in at the lake, and enjoyed so much a good life together. With both of us extremely busy; he as a bus driver and me as a firefighter, our time together was limited. Always a great friend. Never ever forgotten.

How Much The Cost
Of The Emotions Of Sudden Loss
By Jerry H. Ball

How much can one man handle,

How much can one woman endure,

How much grief does one parent capture,

How much pain does a brother feel,

How much sadness does a grandparent realize,

How much anger does a friend display,

How much disbelief is there in a small child,

How much to cope with is with those who care,

How much loss is felt by those who loved,

How much emptiness to begin with,

How much healing there Will Be with time,

How much will be "well-remembered"

Of those, and this thing we call Sudden Loss.

MEDICAL – FRIENDS

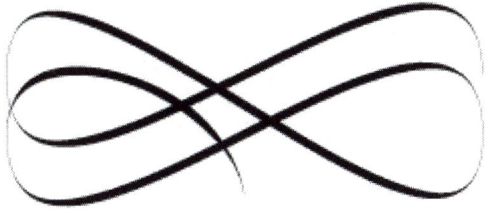

Neighbor, Classmate And Friend

My family and I moved from the house on Golden Avenue out to Fine Lake in the summer of 1959. Along with my stepfather, whom I later called Dad, we spent the first six weeks in a two room tent. With a bathhouse for cleaning and showering, and a trusty Coleman stove, we lived like nomads just 100 yards from the beautiful lake. Our tent was perched on property that had four cabins on it and an incredible sandy beach on the water front. I was playing along the tree line when my mother approached me.

Growing up in a rural setting southeast of downtown Battle Creek, we enjoyed life in the country and yet close to town. My younger sister Gail, and I, were close friends with our next door neighbors, the Willeys. Nancy was my classmate in school and one of my backyard playmates around home. One of our regular activities was neighborhood croquet matches, of which I was pretty decent at.

Nancy enjoyed the camaraderie. We also loved to play kick the can, which is a form of hide and seek, but with a noise factor. You tried to kick it before the one who was "it", touched you. An offshoot of that game was "statue", which when touched, you had to remain still until someone who wasn't "it", touched you and freed you to run around again. It was a joyous time of growing up.

Mom had a serious look on her face. She gently told me that Nancy Willey had died of leukemia, a form of cancer. I was stunned! How does a 12 year old process the death of a former classmate who was the same age? Mom said she was very sorry. As she walked away, I walked around in a fog. How could this happen? There was a hole in me. I couldn't comprehend my world without someone whom I had been so close to; moved away from, and suddenly would never see again. Ever!

Because we lived in such close proximity to one another, for five glorious years we happily shared time with each other. Nancy was my good friend. And now many years later, I am glad I was able to share a part of my young life with her.

Best Friend A Quiet Place

In the summer of 1959, our family moved out to Fine Lake near Battle Creek, Michigan. That's when I first met Roger. We immediately hit it off. Same age; same sense of humor; liked sports and much more. Quickly we were playing catch with a baseball; him teaching me the game of chess, and helping me start a stamp collection. We practically lived on the water, and enjoyed pulling each other water skiing. We were almost inseparable.

After two years of community college, he and I went our separate ways. Eventually Roger got married and returned to his beloved Fine Lake in a new home. Several tragic and painful events were suddenly hovering over him like a plague. He went to bed that night, alone and in deep despair. What did he have to live for now that his wife had passed away, and soon an even bigger calamity would be ready to gobble him up.

Roger was always a lot of fun. We had many good friends together, but mostly we enjoyed our own time together growing up. He continued collecting stamps on a serious level into his later adult years. And he really enjoyed his granddaughter; taking her on trips with the family. We never seemed to find much time for each other after both of us were married. But occasional golf outings or a movie, really meant a lot to me.

Being alone is one of the most difficult experiences a human being can go through. Especially if you've been active your whole life, the transition to being by yourself for much of your days and nights, can lead to physical and mental problems. Without support, the results can be devastating. Roger supposedly took his medicine before retiring – alone in his upstairs bedroom. His son came home, but didn't check on his dad because he said he thought he was asleep. Maybe he should have checked on him.

When morning came, Roger had passed away. No one would reveal the exact cause of death. He had suffered through some trials that had taken a heavy toll on him; suggesting to me that he might have given up – his will to go on. They did an investigation, but the results were never revealed to me.

I miss my friend greatly. I will always remember our trips to Lake Michigan; little league baseball; our undefeated football team; science projects; all night auto theatre movies, and most of all a friendship that cannot ever be matched.

To Suffer No More

Cystic Fibrosis is a devastating disease that always results in death at an early age. Usually the victim dies before the age of 18. But with advances in science, Laura and her family were positive that a cure for her was just around the corner. She was always optimistic about life, and one year came out to play baseball on my daughter Dulcie's team at Wattles Park .

Because of her condition, she couldn't put out the same effort that the other girls did. But as a coach, I am the consummate encourager and teacher. Winning a game is nice. But enjoying and learning to play the game is so much more rewarding. I was working at the fire department when the telephone rang. It was not good news.

Laura enjoyed life to the fullest; the best she could. Limited in doing a lot of things, she continued to fight. Her parents consistent pounding on her back to loosen up her breathing, helped her move on. The support she received from family; her church family, and classmates, made life bearable. News of a possible breakthrough cure gave Laura new hope. Living beyond the age of most children with the disease, she continued to fight and to hope.

Dulcie was on the other end of the line. She asked me if I had heard the sad news and I told her no, I hadn't. Several days later, Dulcie asked if I could go with her to Laura's funeral. There's nothing like attending the funeral for a small child or young person still in their teens, or even early 20's. It's one of the hardest events that the parents of the child, or another parent of any child, can go through. Your emotions reach a new level of low, and understanding how it happened, is difficult if not impossible to grasp.

Unbeknownst to me, I would be attending the funeral for another 19 year old in just a matter of months. It wouldn't be a disease that would take the life of this young woman, but an unselfish act of caring, and a careening car off a slippery road, that would be responsible. In just a few short months, it would be my daughter Dulcie's funeral that I would have to attend. Sudden Loss doesn't have favorites. It's never partial. We must always be prepared to deal with the unexpected in this life. For the very life we're given, is but a gift for just a little while. We must cherish it for all we're worth!

Reflections

Friendship is one of the most special things we possess. When I lost my best friend in Roger, there was a deep vacuum in my life. We had done so much together and now there were but memories. For other friends, there's always a void in your life for a long time when they've left you.

A Personal Glimpse of...

A Personal Glimpse of...
Steve Holston – My High School Buddy

So much of what high school is about is how we react to the situations that arise and the people we associate with on a day to day basis. Steve wasn't one of those classmates who most people really noticed. He was a blend-in kind of guy who didn't want attention drawn to himself. Soft spoken and very much an unassuming personality with low self-esteem, it was a remarkable morning when he approached me in the hallway and loudly proclaimed in an excited voice that he had made the Delton Kellogg high school basketball team. The look on his face was priceless. I'd never seen him so excited!

Even as one of his few true friends in school, Steve rarely spoke of his everyday life away. I knew his younger brother who was very much the opposite in personality. Very outgoing, confident and popular with his peers. He always had good grades hovering around an A.

I don't ever remember seeing Steve dance. Sometimes he'd attend one of the Friday night school dances, but would stand alone usually in a corner somewhere. We'd talk a little, but I was usually out on the floor so our conversations were brief. At other school functions he'd put on a timid smile and speak pleasantly when spoken to but never very outgoing. To me he was the quiet friend who had some deep secrets down inside himself that I'd never ever know about. What I did know for certain was that his brother was the one receiving attention from his family and peers.

It was a really difficult day for me when an extremely forlorn looking Steve Holston approached me in the hallway at school that Monday morning and quietly announced that he had been suspended from the basketball team for low grades. He would have several weeks to raise them up to be eligible for reinstatement. I told him how sorry I was and tried to encourage him saying that I was sure he'd be back on the team soon. I could never have known what devastating emotional effects that his suspension had on him.

I have been so blessed in my life with good people who have made my life better. Steve and I were friends. He absolutely left a lasting impression on me and his legacy will be with me everlasting.

SUICIDE – FRIENDS

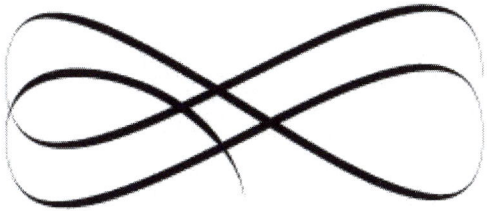

Something Very Wrong The Last To See

I began attending Delton Kellogg schools in the fifth grade. I don't remember the first year I had class with Steve, but I remember him as a fairly quiet and plain looking boy. He was always a little overweight. His brother was much the opposite. Outgoing; nice looking, and quite popular with his classmates. The pressures of not being more like his brother, according to his parents, really bothered him. This was a fact I didn't know.

Steve seemed like a fairly happy boy. He was an average to below average student, but seemed to really cheer up when he found out he had actually made the basketball team in our sophomore year. It was nice having him on the team, but he was not very talented at the sport. He often was picked on by the bullies in school. And yet he seemed to be able to fend off his emotions for the most part, and not let it bother him too much. Or so it seemed.

Steve's grades fell below a "C" average, placing him on probation from the team; causing him obvious depression. That Friday, as I was leaving the little coffee shop across the street from the school where I got a snack before it was time for basketball practice, I saw Steve walking away from me on the street. He looked terrible; his face was totally pale; head hanging down. As I approached him and called out his name, he stopped walking briefly but wouldn't look at me. I asked him if he was alright.

A chill came over me as I tried to look at his eyes. In a quiet and sad voice, he replied that he was "okay", but it was hard to believe him. Now I was really concerned. I asked him if he wanted to talk. He told me, "No, that's alright", and walked away from me traveling north towards his house. That would be the last time I would see him. Something seemed terribly wrong but I didn't know what. I convinced myself that Steve would be alright. On Monday morning, I was told the terrible news and realized how wrong I was.

Steve had arrived home to an empty house; his parents at work; brother still at school. He wrote a note for his brother: - Do Not come down in the basement for anything. Curious, his brother discovered the body hanging from the ceiling. A lot of people attended the funeral; a real tribute to a young man who was really loved and just didn't know it. Maybe we should all have tried harder.

A Man And His Deepest Burden

Life presents itself to each of us in many wondrous ways throughout our lives. So do life's pressures and difficulties. An older man with so much to live for or so it seemed to all those around him. An adoring wife; a house on the lake; a good job for years, and friends. But to him, was all this a façade?

What must he have been going through his mind in the days before the most important and definitive decision of his life.

His wife Joyce, one of my mother's favorite friends, and he enjoyed our family's company. Doing things together often, the four of them (including Dad), would savor life at the lake and other activities as a group.

On a seemingly average day in which Joyce had errands to run, she could see that her husband was at peace with just staying home. A friendly goodbye / I'll see you later was probably spoken and then Joyce backed the car out of the driveway. There were no warning signs. Yes he had recently had some stresses in his life, but nothing that would be out of the ordinary for any of us it seemed.

It was eerily quiet when Joyce returned home late that afternoon. Unlocking the front door and then retrieving several packages from the car, she entered the house. Something didn't feel right. Why was it so quiet she thought?

She began looking for her husband. And then she opened the bedroom door.

Tom enjoyed hunting and fishing. He owned several rifles. On the floor next to the bed was one of those rifles and the unthinkable. She could not keep her emotions from echoing the agony she now had filling her entire being.

It would never be the same in that little house on the lake again. For my mother's dear friend, being alone there would now be her existence. Having good friends, she would carry on. In time, anguished thoughts would fade. But the vivid and horrible memory of that day, and that moment, would haunt her till' her days here on earth were done many years later.

Bridge For A Troubled Life

Sometimes it's hard to know why. So many questions. Sometimes no answers. A young man ponders his life. Maybe he thinks there's no way out. Maybe he feels he's not worth anything. Maybe he's been bullied for a long time. Whatever the reasons, my son's friend decided that he didn't want to be here anymore. I found out about it after the fact. Still, it haunted me to think that there was no one there to save him.

The overpass was busy with vehicles traveling over the top of a very busy freeway. Maybe he pondered awhile whether he should follow through with his plan. Maybe he was fearful; at peace; unsure or completely confident.

We will never know for certain. What is certain, is that the young man climbed the railing and j.............

I was so very sad. For my son. For his friend's family. This young man - as are with all young people, full of promise that maybe even they

131

don't know or comprehend. Was there someone who could have prevented what happened on this day? Another question that probably no one will ever be able to answer.

Reflections

I'm not certain how anyone who's left behind when another takes their own life can react other that with extreme anxiety or unspeakable shock. When I lost my classmate Steve, there was deep sorrow and disbelief on my part. I had just spoken to him that same day. And then the horrific news was given to us on Monday morning when we got to class. It was unbelievably and indescribably unbelievable!

SUICIDE – FIRE DEPARTMENT

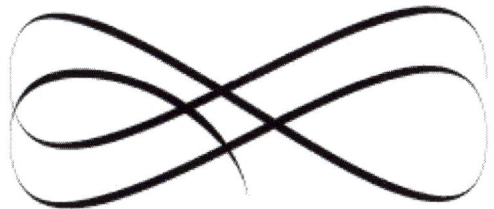

A Mothers Love And Deep Despair

There are some calls on the fire department that are upsetting right from the start. This was one of them. A reported attempted suicide by hanging on Territorial Road in Battle Creek. Engine 4 arrived on the scene that afternoon not knowing what we'd find. An elderly man thought he saw something strange in his neighbor's basement and called 911. We got the front door open and went inside. There were no lights on, but we were able to locate the basement door without any problem.

The lieutenant and I started down the stairs when we both looked to our left and saw something hanging from the floor joists. It was a young woman. He told me to go back upstairs and wait for the ambulance crew. He didn't want to disturb the area in case it was a crime scene.

As I stood in the kitchen, the ambulance crew arrived and came into the house. One, a man, was a seasoned veteran. His partner, a young woman just out of training, was all pumped up to do her job. They rushed down the stairs and found my lieutenant, and the body.

She immediately rushed back up the stairs as fast as she could and came up to me white as a sheet. She wasn't ready for the reality of this scene. The look of the body was nothing like I'd ever seen before either. I totally understood the young ambulance attendant's reaction. It was horrible!

The young woman in the basement, in her late 20's to early 30's, had become desperate. Trying to support herself and her 12 year old daughter; working a job she absolutely hated, she had called her mother to have her take the daughter somewhere for a few hours so she could take care of some things.

Nearly 20 notes addressed to people important to her were setting neatly on a small table nearby in the basement. Her plan had succeeded. But the pain it left behind was immeasurable.

So Witty - So Sad

There was always a cheery, non-smiling hello from Dave when I entered #2 Fire Station. He was a truck guy who loved the ladder truck and had been an accomplished driver and operator for years. It almost seemed his calling. He loved guns and would often show off some of the many he owned. With his retirement, came the end of an era. A coffee hour and then time to do whatever he pleased.

He had a troubled side to him other than what most people witnessed on a day to day basis. And one day he decided that this world was too much to handle. One of his own guns took his life. I wish I could have talked him out of it. I had no idea he would ever think of doing such a thing.

She Couldn't Take It

How do we deal with a painful illness? How about more than one at a time? While on the fire department, we were dispatched to Lois Avenue on the south side of town. We were informed that a next door neighbor could see exhaust coming from the closed garage door for quite some time. He was concerned and called 911.

We opened the access door and found the car running. An older woman was lying on the floor partially underneath the rear end of the vehicle by the exhaust pipe. She had decided that life was much too hard. We took the time to console her husband. These medical runs were always very difficult.

Reflections

While working as a firefighter, I saw many difficult things. Most however paled in comparison to seeing a human being who didn't really look like one anymore. One of the most awful visuals in my life happened when we were first on the scene and I came upon the victim who looked so unlike the young person she once was. O' the sorrow her family must have felt. Such was her life that she felt she could no longer hold on. For her, hope was evidently gone. All of us desperately need hope.

FIRE – FIRE DEPARTMENT

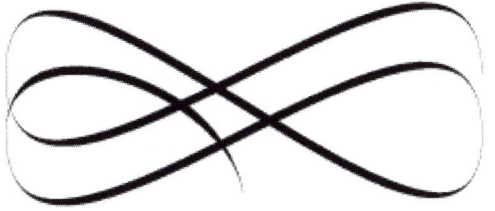

A Raging Fire - Incomprehensible Loss

While on the fire department, I was a member of "B" shift. We were allowed to fill in on other shifts either because of overtime or if we exchanged time with another firefighter; filling in for him or her on their shift. On an evening when all had been quiet while working on "C" shift, the alarm suddenly sounded; a reported house fire on Grove Street.

When we arrived on the scene, the house was engulfed in flames. I was the pump operator on Engine 2 which was staged nearby on another street. The first fire vehicles on the scene were already pumping water.

As fire operations continued, the fire department was alerted with a safety message that two small children might still be inside. What suddenly seemed like a routine empty house fire, became a rescue operation and everyone on the scene went into a totally different mode. The fire hampered any concerted effort to locate the children until after it was knocked down.

The mother of the two children was casually walking back down the street towards home, when she realized all the emergency vehicles were in front of her house. In her absence, the children had been left unattended. That's when tragedy struck.

At a distance from the actual scene, I received the horrible news. With my children being small, an anguish filled my stomach and an aching in my heart. How could anyone just up and leave their two small children all by themselves? If the question is ever raised, "What could go wrong? I'm only going to be gone a few minutes". On a dark night on Grove Street, the answer was given.

To Rise And Fall

We're taught to stop, drop and roll during a fire. But that's if you know there is one. An elderly woman goes to bed early. Unbeknownst to her, a fire is starting in another room. Because it's winter, the house is sealed up tight. A neighbor notices light smoke coming from the house and immediately calls 911. The fire department arrives on the scene. When there's no answer at the door and smoke showing, the door is forced open.

Percentage wise, a fire needs more oxygen to free burn than we need to breathe. So when the fire depletes the oxygen to a certain level, the fire looks to go out. But it is truly just waiting for oxygen to be reintroduced into the atmosphere. When the door was opened, air rushed in and the fire exploded all throughout the house.

The woman finally woke up to the noise, and when she stood up from her bed, the intense heat instantly seared her lungs causing her to immediately collapse. She was gone. The next morning, with the shift change, we were dispatched to help remove the body. You could see the outline of her body on the bed and footprints on the floor. It was something I'll never forget.

No Chance To Get Out

It was a seemingly normal night for the family of four in their home on Spencer Street in Battle Creek. The two story house had a center staircase and at the top were the bedrooms. The two small children slept on the north side of the house with the parent's room down the hall on the south side.

When the explosion rocked the house, it instantly woke up the father. The ensuing fire quickly spread. The man left his wife's side and rushed in to attempt to save the children. He reached the children's room and came back out, but made it only to the top of the stairs where he collapsed. The fire took total control until city fire units finally doused the last of the flames. The grim task of recovering the family lay ahead.

It is so difficult for the average citizen to understand how fireworks. Almost never is it the flames that kill. The super-heated smoke and gases are the main culprit. This particular fire shocked the whole community.

B.L.E.V.E. - Horrific Sudden Explosion

In the fire department, we had a wide variety of training. From fire rescue and fire suppression to water rescue and multiple medical emergency scenarios. During my first year on the department, we filed into the training room early one morning and the training officer announced that we would be watching the training film, "B.L.E.V.E." (Boiling Liquid Expanding Vapor Explosion)

It was 1981 and the film, which was quite old, was made by a member of the media. The fire scene was somewhere along the eastern seaboard. There was a train derailment and several of the tanker cars were leaking and a fire ensued under one of the cars.

Multiple departments were dispatched with a total of 50 plus firefighters on the scene. A ladder truck was set up with the deck gun flowing a large volume of water high above the tank car that was on fire. Several firefighters were positioned on the ladder. Others were near the control panel of the truck and all around the scene as it unfolded.

While watching the film, I was relaxed and excited because I was now a real firefighter. I was fascinated by all the activity going on as efforts were being made to bring the fire under control and secure the scene; making it safe for railroad workers to do their job. Then suddenly...............

You can see the firefighter on the end of the extended ladder operating the deck gun, and others on the ground. Without warning, there was a loud hissing sound, and then - KA BOOOOOOOOOOMMM!!!! In the blink of an eye; a split second; over 20 firefighters lost their lives. It was hard to believe what I was watching.

Over the course of my many years on the department, the vivid memory of that training film helped me be a safer firefighter; always aware of the dangers that lurk on any fire scene.

Reflections

Few things compared during my time in the fire department than to see, hear and feel the effects of fire on a human being. None for me was more evident and traumatic than the night on Grove Street. While standing beside my pumper, I hear the safety message that behind the massive flames, two small children are unaccounted for. That night changed me forever.

WEATHER

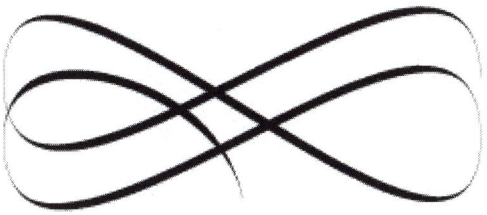

The Terror Plunging Down

The majesty and beauty of the Mackinaw Bridge defies description. On warm sunny days, the drive across is a delight; a positive adventure. But during storms, it is not the preferable place to be. With 80 – 100 mile per hour winds sometimes howling around and through the grated roadway, you must use extreme caution when venturing out at these treacherous times.

She was late! And even though the wind was blowing with great intensity, something inside her told her that she must take a chance and cross the big bridge. Driving a tiny Yugo is quite an experience in itself. Great gas mileage and able to zip around in traffic, it was a very popular ride for the younger generation. But in a storm, some choices are not the best ones.

The young woman began to speed across. With the caution sign lit, other vehicles were few on the bridge this dark night. The wind howled and the bridge was swaying as she reached the halfway point on the 5-mile span crossing the great lakes at the point where Lake Michigan and Lake Huron meet.

Even more violently now, the wind began to alter the little cars stability. And then suddenly, and without warning, it blew the car to the side curb and then violently over the railing. Plummeting several hundred feet straight down and then plunging into the icy waters below, never to be seen again. I've been across the bridge. The young woman's decision to cross under these conditions still haunts me. Was anything that important?

Terror From The Sky

It was a humid day. The children in the elementary school were enjoying their time in class. The teachers were well prepared for a disaster, and performed several drills each year. The clouds began to gather and the skies became ugly.

And then, without warning, a huge funnel cloud came crashing down on the community. It was heading right for the school. The teachers got the children out into the hallway as they had practiced so many times before. But this time, everything was for real.

It hit right in the middle of the school building. Tornadoes don't pick and choose whose lives they'll take. Small children died that day. A sad, sad day indeed. I've been through several tornadoes in my lifetime and it's just about the scariest thing to witness and be a victim to. My heart went out to all those little people, teachers and families who went through one terrible afternoon when terror came from the sky.

Helpless - A Black Monster

I'd been through a tornado at Fine Lake when I was young. That same year, I witnessed mass destruction from one at Coldwater Lake. The sound is indescribable. The complete changing of a landscape is hard to fathom. It was all of this in 1963.

It is now years later. While at the VA Medical Center in Battle Creek, I enjoyed my job working in the Engineering department. As late afternoon approached on a warm and humid day, I looked forward to getting out of work and heading into town to pay some bills.

Looking out the window from my office around 4 pm, I could see the clouds gathering. It grew eerily dark with the sky now a sickening greenish-gray. The sky then quickly blackened and suddenly the strong wind was gone. There was not a sound. Dead silence!

Just like years before, no birds were chirping; no dogs barking; nothing. Then came the hail; the wind began to whip up and the huge trees on the campus began swaying violently. I quickly rushed out to my car to try and beat the storm. I must get to downtown today I told myself. What I didn't know, was that just a few miles to the west, a huge tornado was tearing into the small town of Augusta.

Already causing massive damage in Kalamazoo and killing 5 people, the storm was moving quickly – right towards the VA complex. I quickly drove my Pinto towards the west entranceway to the VA. Suddenly, no matter how I tried, the car would not move forward. With blackness all around, and trees seemingly ready to crash down on me at any moment, I realized I had made a terrible mistake. Only God could save me now.

The storm did pass; the tornado dissipated into the air, and the sky began to clear. With rain still pelting down, and visibly shaken, I was finally able to drive once more. Moving forward, I headed for Battle Creek.

This was not my first encounter with a tornado. What I didn't know at the time, was that it also would not be my last.

Unbelievably Wrong

It was extremely hot outside when she parked her car at the beauty salon. She didn't have a babysitter, so the three kids would just have to go along. This wouldn't take too long; telling the children to behave and not get out of the car for any reason. Even though it was nearing 90 degrees outside, she rolled up the windows all but a little and locked the doors. Then she went inside.

Having gone to this salon for years, she enjoyed talking to the beauticians who worked there. When you're talking and laughing while getting your hair done, the time seems to slip by so quickly. Besides, it's air conditioned and feels really good. It took longer than she expected for her perm.

Hours had gone by when the woman exited the building. Why didn't she see the kids in the car? O' they were there. They just weren't responsive when she unlocked the door to the sweltering insides. The emergency workers knew what had happened. There was no saving to be done.

As I read about this, I became really angry and sick to my stomach. How could ANYONE be so reckless and thoughtless when it comes to your children? For this woman, the cost was immeasurable!

Reflections

I cannot imagine the paralyzing fear she must have felt in those blizzard conditions on the big bridge. Just thinking about it brings back a visual in my mind of ultimate horror and there's nothing that you can do. Even more traumatic for me personally, was to be right in the path of a massive tornado with no escape possible but by the grace of God himself.

DROWNING – PERSONAL

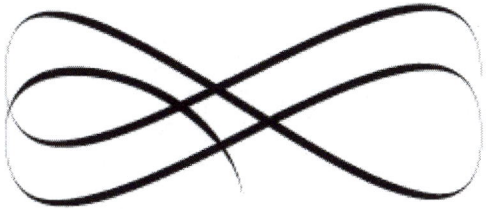

A Life's Reality - The Water Defined

It's funny how you can be in high school for four years and not really get to know some of your classmates well. For me, Mary was one of those. She was very quiet and studious; someone who normally didn't stick out in a crowd. She was always nice when you'd talk to her, but had little to say during a conversation.

I saw her on several occasions after high school working at the local drug store in Urbandale – a suburb of Battle Creek. She told me that after graduating from college, most businesses wouldn't hire her because she was over qualified. Not too long after our last visit, I found out some really disturbing news that still haunts me to this day.

It was on our senior trip that I got to know Mary on a personal level. Delton Kellogg High is a small school just northwest of Battle Creek. Having the largest graduating class in school history at 100, made us proud. But there was a lot of indecision as to where to take our senior trip.

So while most of the class took the weekend off, 16 of us headed for Detroit to catch a ferry boat for a three day excursion on Lake Huron and an exciting day on Mackinac Island. Four of us, including my best friend Roger, Mary and one other classmate, toured the island together; rode bikes around the island, and spent a glorious weekend together. Lots of laughter and getting to know one another better.

Several years later, we had our five year class reunion. I didn't recall Mary being there, and every now and then wondered how she was. It wasn't too long after that, that Roger told me the news that still troubles me. According to the reports, Mary, who had seizures, was taking a bath when one of them struck. She probably didn't realize what was happening to her as she slipped underneath the water.

Even though we only got to know each other during a much happier time over a single weekend, I'm so glad that Mary was one person who left such a profound impact on my life. She made my life better.

Such A Beautiful Little Child

When I was in high school, I was infatuated by a young girl who sat two rows over from me in one of my classes. Her name was Cindy. She was a grade below me, so this was the only class we had together. I didn't realize at the time that my friend Pete, also noticed her in school at the beginning of our junior year. I asked her out on a date several times and we had so much in common that I thought for sure she would become my girlfriend.

Though we really enjoyed each other's company, she had her eye on Pete. Cindy and I stayed friends all through school. She once wrote a little book of poetry for me, which I treasured.

After high school, Cindy and Pete got married and had a child – a little girl.

I lost track of both of them for many years, but never forgot the all-American girl I so enjoyed being with. Then one day, Pete returned to Michigan with a new woman in his life that he planned on marrying in the near future. He invited me over to their house, and we talked about a lot of things. He and Cindy had divorced; in part because of a tragedy that had happened years before.

On a sunny and warm afternoon, Cindy had taken the little 4-year-old out into the back yard to play. The couple had a small swimming pool filled with water, and so the child was excited to be able to cool off in it. According to Pete, her mother became distracted and went into the house, leaving their daughter unattended for a short time.

Coming back out into the yard, the little girl was not visible at first. In a panic, Cindy rushed over to the pool to find her child unresponsive and not breathing. In but a moment, my two good friends would have such a traumatic event that changed their lives collectively and then individually.

Tears filled my eyes as he briefly told me the story. Not one to ever show much emotion, I could tell by his facial expression, that this one event affected him more than he would ever let on. I was deeply saddened by what I'd just been told.

With Friends - A Dark Watery Secret

As a member of the fire department, we are trained in water rescue; specifically on the Kalamazoo or Battle Creek rivers or on Goguac Lake. A number of rigs instantly responded when the alarm went off that overcast day and headed downstream from the Ralston cereal plant off Dickman Road. A lot is running through your mind as you are preparing for the task at hand.

Station 5 is the furthest city firehouse from the plant, so we staged the engine on the 20th Street overpass, about a mile downstream. Then we began walking the river on each side, looking for a young boy.

It had been a fun day of playing with his friends. The three adolescent boys, had been walking along the river when they decided to climb onto the little walkway bridge that crossed over the river providing access to the cereal plant. Everything was fine, and then.........

One of the boys fell into the swirling waters of the fast moving river. It would carry him quickly towards the fork where the Battle Creek River merged into the Kalamazoo. Right there is a cauldron of violently churning water from the recent heavy rains in the area.

Many firefighters and other emergency service personnel searched for hours and hours for the missing child. The small villages of Augusta and Galesburg downstream were alerted and the local township department and other volunteers also began searching the river. After several days of looking, including boats and aircraft searching the waters, - Nothing.

The little boy was never found. A professional diver even attempted to go down into the dangerous waters where the two rivers meet and had to be pulled back up by his safety line because the river was too violent. We eventually went back to the station and waited to hear news about the boy. Sadly none ever came.

In The Murky, Dark Lake

Halfway between Fine Lake where I lived and Hickory Corners, Michigan, there is a small lake that fishermen love. And in the summer, people will sometimes stop at the boat landing and dive in to cool off.

Some would say that this was a bottomless lake; that sometimes things would go in and never return. There was a raft on the lake the day four visitors decided to go for a swim. One of them was a very large and heavy set man who had limited swimming experience.

With two of them swimming out, the heavy set man finally reached the raft and then dove deep into the water. His swimming partner was setting on the raft by then and waited for him pop up. I used to dive deep off a raft into Fine Lake. There was always a little bit of fear in going near the bottom in the weeds. You had to be careful not to get tangled up in them.

The man never resurfaced. The one on the raft searched the water for him, but when he still couldn't find him, swam back to shore and they went for help. A long and thorough search was conducted including a highly skilled professional skin diver. To this day the man's body was never recovered.

Reflections

We searched and searched relentlessly for the young man who had accidentally fallen into the raging rivers waters. To have every resource available searching and coming up empty, there's not much of a worse feeling for a professional who's supposed to be able to solve problems and make for happy endings. For the family, not knowing is still the worst part.

ANIMAL ATTACK

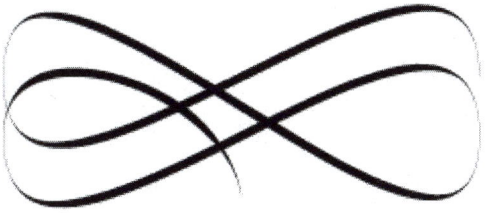

A Spring Morning - A Precious Friend Lost

She was one of a kind! Each day that I would enter the building, she would greet me in her own special way. There would always be a lot of noise here, and each one of her room mates, acted like they hadn't been fed in forever. But I guess when you have minimal brain capacity and the rooster leading you out of the coop is annoying as usual, rushing to get outside for breakfast makes all of this chaos tolerable.

I called her Biddy. She was my chicken. No I didn't cuddle her, or even pick her up. But something about her was special to me. Besides, I was only about 6 years old, and chickens, and roosters were sort of imposing creatures what with their beaks and sharp talons and all.

I stood looking out the screen door at the back of the house on a beautiful, warm, spring morning. The sun was sort of hazy, and as I looked across the driveway at Grandpa and Grandma's house, something caught the corner of my right eye. Movement. An animal coming down the long driveway. A large animal; black I think, now coming into clear view. It had something in its mouth. That something was white with thin black stripes, and an orange beak.

As the large black dog trotted directly in front of me, my face suddenly showed the horror that I now felt. In his mouth was a chicken, my little mind quickly processed. But not just Any chicken; IT WAS BIDDY!!!

I could not hold back the tears and the sadness I was feeling. How could that awful animal do such a terrible thing? My mother tried everything to console me. But it took a long, long time before I could once again enter that chicken coop. My friend was gone. My first Sudden Loss – a stark reality.

Years later, while visiting at my son's home and pseudo farm in Virginia, I was asked to feed his twenty-plus chickens. For some reason, one of the chickens would always be the first one coming up to me. It was white with thin black stripes. She seemed special amongst all the other clucking birds.

167

I gave it some thought one evening on the porch as she ate out of my hand. Chuckling to myself, I decided she needed a name. I told myself that her name would be B----! How original.

Innocence So Quickly Gone

She just went out to play in her fenced in yard. Her mother was comfortable with letting her little 4 year old girl out to play where she could watch from the window. Two houses over, the neighbors had two pit bull dogs. Never a problem before, and with two sets of fences between the two yards, everything seemed safe. It was, until this particular morning.

With the little girl playing in the grass, something in the dogs caused them to become suddenly and unexpectedly aggressive. Some statistics put the rate of all dog attacks; 60% are from pit bulls . The two animals leaped over two 4-foot chain link fences and viciously attacked and killed the little girl. No one could pull them off before it was too late. So sudden. So very sad!

The dogs were put to sleep. This breed of dog was trained a long time ago to be aggressive; man's doing. Is there an easy answer on how to prevent such devastating events? No. My heart cried out when I read the article.

Three Times - And Harm

She had lived in her apartment for quite some time. A man across the hall owned 2 pit bulls. They were always aggressive acting when they would see someone coming out of their apartment. All the tenants were concerned for their own safety. On two separate occasions, she was locking her door as she prepared to leave, when his door opened and he and his two dogs came out into the hallway. The dogs lunged and barked at her; one time nearly knocking her down before the man could pull them back.

She called the police to file a complaint, but because nothing had happened, there wasn't anything they could do. Now fearing greatly for her safety, she would be extremely cautious whenever leaving her apartment to be sure the neighbor and his dogs weren't coming out at the same time.

The woman had to leave for work early one morning, so she cautiously checked the hallway and it was clear. As she locked her door, the neighbor and the 2 pit bulls suddenly appeared. The dogs lunged at the woman and got loose from their owner. They literally tore the woman apart. The dogs were destroyed; the owner now due in court.

So what should the public do in situations like this? What are the options? This woman is often on my mind. It is disturbing that this had to happen!

Reflections

As a little boy, I was devastated at my pet's demise. Life provides these catastrophes when we're young so that we can handle the more important ones later on. But when someone's pets are the cause of the needless destruction of a human being, as an adult I am torn apart inside. People with animals that are this aggressive, must be more responsible and considerate for the welfare of those around them.

ANIMAL – PERSONAL

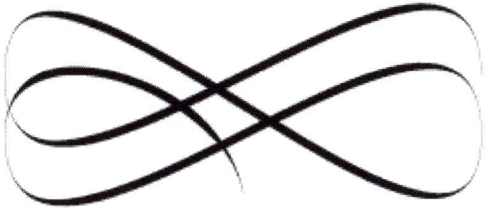

A Most Difficult Decision

Each day when my time on the Army base was over, around 5 o'clock, I would head home in the Texas heat. Living in a house trailer with my wife and infant son, we were doing pretty well.

We loved animals. There was a couple who lived two doors down. He was also in the service, so your living status is never secure.

They had a female German Shepherd who recently had puppies. Giving two away early, the other two enjoyed playing in the yard while tied to a post. When the third puppy found a home, the last one seemed lonely. Still, every day when I came home, he would leap and bark at me in a happy way.

I hadn't seen the neighbors in a couple of weeks. The little dog continued to greet me with his jumping and happy bark. He was such an energetic little guy. Then one afternoon as I walked up to my trailer, I looked over and the dog wasn't moving much; just sitting; looking at me. The next few days were the same. I finally went over to check on the little dog and noticed a coarse rope had cut deeply into his neck. He could barely breathe.

It was one of the most difficult decisions I ever had to make. The vet said it would be extremely expensive to treat him and couldn't guarantee his survival because of the infection. He was suffering terribly. Shortly thereafter, I made the difficult decision to put him out of his misery. The owners had moved without notice and weren't coming back.

My Pets - My Family

I'm like a lot of people. Pets are an important part of my life; my family. And when they die, I'm deeply saddened at the loss of a furry friend. One of the most difficult tasks in my life, was what I had to do for a dog that had traveled from Texas with my family upon my discharge from the Army.

Shy was a good dog. Part Collie and Shepherd, he was small in stature and a good watch dog. On a Christmas Eve night, he went over our chain length fence and began roaming the neighborhood while we were away. Upon returning home, we pulled up into the driveway and immediately noticed Shy on our steps with a severely injured leg.

With an emergency operation, and a steel wire put in, he healed and lived a good life with us. But as time went on, he began to nip at other animals and then at people. Soon he would want to viciously attack passing dogs in the street. A most difficult decision to have him put down was made.

I took him on a Saturday to a vet clinic far away. I couldn't do it locally. He wiggled and jumped on me excitedly when we went inside. I agonized over what I was about to do. Finally, they brought me the papers to sign. With everything ready, I said my last tearful goodbye to my good friend. When they told me it was over, I broke down and wept. It was so hard. One moment he's wagging his tale; the next, he's gone from us forever.

Others I've had to do this with were my cats Spunky, Fluffette, and most recently Tigger and Otis. My beloved dog Ferdie was so difficult as well. We also had my young son's gerbil and two guinea pigs die in our hands. There was nothing we could do but comfort them in their last moments.

Reflections

I love children and adore my pets. So when the awful opportunity presented itself in these two cases, I shuttered and cried afterwards. It's sometimes the right thing and the only thing to do. I recently had to complete the task again with a severely injured bird. It does not get easier!.

There Is Hope
By Jerry H. Ball

We never want to lose them. And then, when it happens suddenly and without warning, our sadness and grief overwhelms us initially. We attempt to celebrate their life at a gathering, but we're crying inside. The reality is – they are no longer here with us.

But hope then raises its head from our emotional ashes, and a little ray of sunshine peaks out from within' our heart. We remember things about them; mostly happy things, that makes this sudden and drastic chaos more bearable.

Then time begins to complete its task of healing us. It's never an easy course we'll follow. But as "this time" extends itself; from moments after the last gathering of family, friends and acquaintances, until weeks and months have passed by ever more quickly, do our emotions begin to settle.

Years will pass too. The first – the most difficult! A first anniversary. Maybe getting together with family and friends; those closest to you. And then, another year, and after that, the many years. And soon the pain eases its worksome path. There are so many things and so many other people who fill our lives; making us full and alive once more.

O' not that we should ever forget that loved one – that friend. This isn't likely to happen! But we shall continue on for all of those still around us who, like those who have passed from this world, made our lives, and make our lives still, a very good and special place to be in. And God too, who has always been there through it all, gives us renewed strength and purpose to live on and to live well.

And to that person of Sudden Loss we say: "There will always be some very special memories we'll cherish forever. You made our lives more complete. We miss and love you. You will never be forgotten!"

SHOOTINGS – THE MASSES

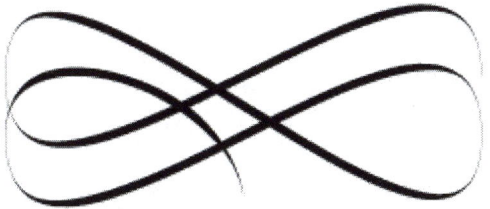

Two Young Men, Bullying And Chaos

Working at Fire Station #6 in Battle Creek the morning I heard the breaking news on television, I was in shock. There had been other shootings at schools before, but none on the scale of this one.

One thinks of Colorado as out of the way for a mass murder. But does this devious act have to have a particular, more familiar and likely place it likes to surface? Absolutely not! It was on this day that two very unhappy and angry young high school students walked into their high school and without warning, began shooting anyone and everyone they could.

They were angry at being bullied; at being made fun of because they were different. And after months of others belittling and berating them, these two decided on a pact. They knew they wouldn't make it out of the building once their actions had begun. They only knew that they were going to set the stage and then play it out to the end.

When one student was asked by one of the killers if she believed in God and she said yes, he told her that she was going to meet him. She stood on her principles and it ended her life. I could not believe what I was seeing live on television. My thoughts immediately jumped to my own high schoolers and their safety.

Months later, supposedly a joke, a "hit list" of students at Harper Creek High School who would be targeted, had my daughter's name on it. The ultimate reality of what might happen; what could happen, came alive in me. Our world in the United States changed dramatically that morning in Colorado.

I sent copies of the song I wrote for my nephew Jason, "It Seems They Left Too Soon" to Columbine High School in hopes that in some way, it might help the families of this horrendous tragedy.

179

December Present - Tragedy Beyond Measure

The day was dreary and gray outside. For me, a house painter doing interior work in Kalamazoo, the weather was fine. With a radio to keep me company, I enjoyed listening to my Christian radio station and the great songs of Christmas. I'm thinking as I'm painting the living room about the grandchildren and the fun this season will be.

And then they interrupted the broadcast to announce that there was a mass shooting at the Sandy Hook Elementary School in New Town, Connecticut.   I stopped what I was doing; stared out the picture window, and began to have tears well up in my eyes.

It started out as a normal day with the children coming into the school with excitement in their talking and actions. It was nearly Christmas, and every child seemed to sense that the upcoming vacation time was almost here. They were all now settled in their classrooms to begin the day.

Suddenly, a young man with a weapon, broke into the school and quickly confronted the principle; shooting her and then many of the first and second graders in their classrooms. He then turned the gun on himself and it was suddenly over.

The bravery of the teachers who died protecting their children; the other children hiding away so the killer couldn't get to them. So many stories to follow; so much grief to bear! The parents of the children at the school were immediately notified, and very quickly, terrified moms and dads showed up hoping and praying that their child wasn't one of the children who were killed. I agonized with them from a very long distance away. There will always be questions that will remain; the biggest one – WHY?

An Evil Design

Some of the most incomprehensible plans of destruction are just mind boggling! Even worse, is when an individual convinces a child that what he's about to do, is alright. It began with a plan to modify an older model car by cutting a hole in the trunk to see out and fire a weapon through. With the plan put into action, the wounding and killing began.

I was going on a trip to Virginia to see my son. I was aware that a shooter was on a killing spree. So when I stopped at a gas station to fill up, I was always ducking and moving around to prevent me from becoming a target for this unstable assassin. The killing continued.

Then at a rest stop, a visitor there noticed the older model car parked in the lot. He notified the authorities who quickly moved in and arrested an older man and his young accomplice. The killing stopped. And I was left wondering how anyone could use people as sport. Sometimes the evil of man makes no sense. I thought, I could have been a target; a victim. It's good that it was finally over.

Reflections

Some of my most difficult losses have come with the splash of media and the thought that someone could kill innocent children without any remorse. And to sit alongside a highway and target practice on human beings takes the lack of a conscious to a whole new level.

SHOOTINGS – PERSONALIZED

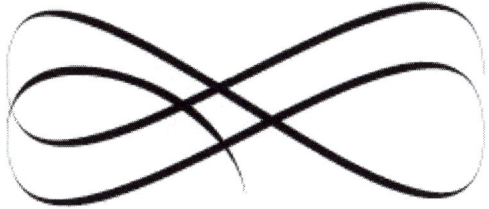

The Nerves Gave In

The National Guard provides this country with an amazing force to help secure difficult situations and bring security and peace back to an area. But in one instance, the minimal training one particular unit had in riot control, did not serve them or the community well.

It was a turbulent time. Kent State, Ohio was a college town. With protests going on all over the country, no one could have predicted the deadly outcome on this day. With college kids anxious and upset over what was going on in their country, and especially our involvement in Viet Nam, they decided to do something about it. And so they gathered en mass and let the administration and the country know they were very unhappy.

The National Guard was called in. With full riot gear on, they were deployed to the protest area. Their nerves were on end, as some of the protesters began throwing things and insults at the armed soldiers. Then, something went terribly wrong.

One story is that one of the guardsmen thought shots had been fired and so he fired back. Other troops joined in, reacting to the shots being fired, and suddenly college students were fleeing for their lives. Four innocent students were killed. Many others injured.

In this country, we have a right to free speech. We also have the right to be protected. And sometimes things can go terribly wrong between the two.

Everyone's Hero

John F. Kennedy was only in his 40's when he became President of the United States. His wife Jacqueline and he, had two beautiful children.

He was a fantastic speaker, and had great charisma. And along with the aid of his brother Bobby, the Attorney General of the United States, they did a lot to get America physically fit.

In 1962, this country was confronted with a decision that could have started a nuclear war with the Soviet Union in Cuba. Against the advice of his generals, John and Bobby convinced the Premier of Russia to back down. Against all odds, they may have saved the world. Now there was division.

On November 22, 1963, I was in shop class when over the intercom, the terrible news that John F. Kennedy, our President, had been shot and killed in Dallas, Texas. Just 14 at the time, I was a part of dead silence and then sobbing in our classroom. The state funeral really made me sad. It was one of the most difficult times of my young life.

He Made A Difference

His brother was President. He was Attorney General. Together they made really difficult decisions that changed the course of history. They were champions for the Civil Rights Movement; putting a man on the moon; bringing physical education to our schools, and staving off a war in Cuba.

When, in 1968, he announced his candidacy for President, many in this country were starved for what they felt Robert could bring to our nation. While on the campaign trail, a man lay in waiting. And when the time was right, he stood there pointing a gun and ended Robert Kennedy's life.

Again I was deeply saddened by the terrible and sudden loss of one of my hero's. First his brother, and now him. It was speculated that the two brothers decision in the Cuban Missile Crisis were possibly reasons for their assassinations. It hurt me greatly for many years.

He Definitely Had A Good Dream

If the Kennedy's brought pride and courage to this country, Martin Luther King Jr. brought real purpose. For centuries throughout the world, the Black race was considered inferior. The Civil War was a deadly way to finally give men of color their freedom, or sort of. In this country, following World War II, you would find little signs in the 1950's and 60's at a drinking fountain or restroom saying whites only! Not much had changed.

And then along came a family man with a vision. He fought verbally; he led marches; he moved this country like no one before him to recognize that all men are created equal and therefore should have equal opportunities with their white brothers and sisters. He forced the Voters Rights Act into being.

He Made A Difference. I would always follow what he was doing; what he was saying; where he was and who was following him.

Martin Luther King believed that all should share in what this country stands for. Black and White and Everyone. Like the Kennedy's, there were people that did not want their traditional bigotry and prejudiced ways to be infringed upon. One spring day in Memphis, Tennessee, the man who changed America with peaceful intent, was gunned down at a motel. I cried.

It was 1968. Now there were three gone forever.

Reflections

Aren't heroes supposed to live forever? Several of mine certainly did not. A President who gave our country real hope. A prospective President who would have brought new hope. An inspirational leader who was the epitome of what that word means and who truly lived it. Through them, I believed in a better world that we could live in.

TERRORISTS

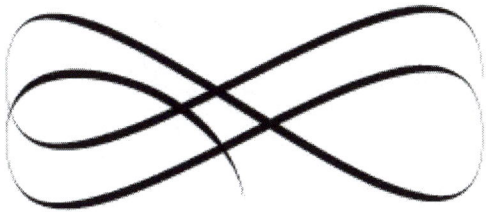

Of Hatred And Revenge

The morning was quiet in Oklahoma City. The sun just coming up and people everywhere going to work. Workers at the federal building were already in the process of doing their jobs. The daycare center was such a blessing for those employees with small children. No one even noticed when the large box truck pulled up in front. No one suspected the driver or his soon to be accomplice as they completed last minute details.

The massive explosion just after 9 am ripped the front of the multi-story building to shreds, including the daycare center. The shock wave was enormous. People were crawling out of their offices; bloodied victims still alive, cried for help; emergency workers and volunteers everywhere trying to save the injured. 168 people died that day. Senselessly. Unfairly. Such cruelty to the innocent I thought. I cried.

A car sped out of the city. The police ensued. Taken into custody – two men who despised the government. Two deranged individuals whose cause dismantled and killed so many. It was gut-wrenching to listen to the newscast. Another sad, sad day in the country I so love.

Terror In The Sky

It was a warm morning as I prepared to leave Battle Creek's #5 Fire Station. Several of the on duty firefighters and I were talking in the parking lot when Gary came out and said, "You guys are going to want to see this"!

Quickly going back into the building and into the sitting room, on television was the image of what looked like a small airplane stuck into the side of one of the World Trade Center Towers. We thought maybe it was a private plane gone off course. When a close-up view was presented, we realized it was not what we thought at all.

191

Not too long after that, a second full sized aircraft rammed into the second tower. That's when the world knew that the United States of America was under attack! Nearly 3000 people died that day, including hundreds of firefighters and other emergency personnel. The biggest surprise attack since World War II had just happened.

As a firefighter and a citizen; and like the rest of the country, I was in shock! At the same time, I could see myself entering those towers and helping people to safety. I would have done it in a second – without hesitation!

Why does the Hate of some cause catastrophe on such a large scale? Did we as a country survive that morning? Of course we did. Will we be attacked again? The probability is almost certain. May God be with this country and the people in it – now and forever.

A Glorious, Horrific Day

The Boston Marathon has always intrigued and fascinated me. I love to run. In high school I was a distance runner, usually the mile run. In college I ran on the Kellogg Community College team; in the Army, all the time. That was all before 1974.

Then in 1981, I was introduced to distance road racing and fell in love with it. After running several 10K events (6.2 miles), I decided to begin training for a marathon. Boston was my first choice. But a series of injuries kept my dream on hold. By the time I was healthy enough, you had to meet their time requirements, which I couldn't do. I decided to run the Detroit Free Press marathon and I finished strong; in the top 30%. 4 hours & 10 minutes.

So when they lined up in 2014 for this past spring's race, I once again got the urge to begin training. My free time is extremely limited, so as yet I've been unable to start. Working, I wasn't able to see the race on

TV. It wasn't until I caught the breaking news. Two explosions; people screaming; running away; runners in a daze; people everywhere in shock; except two very calm young men walking deliberately through the crowd. Two young men: one dies in a gun battle; one is in jail awaiting trial.

Having run a marathon and many, many road races in my life, I cannot imagine what the participants were feeling and dealing with. So many spectators and family and friends at the finish line. My heart went out to the families of the victims and the injured; physically and emotionally. Our time in history has a much added danger factor in all we do here in America.

May we always be vigilant and mindful of what is going on around us.

The Monster Showed His Face

The 1972 Olympics in Munich, Germany were exciting right from the start. The United States track team was picked to win many gold medals. The Israeli team, though small, was primed to win some medals as well. There was security around. But as it turned out, not nearly enough!

Extremists snuck into the Olympic Village and carried out a vicious and deadly assault on the Israeli team, killing most of their country's contingency. It was a sad time; the Olympics; peaceful competition; the world together for sport not politics. Things would never be the same. As an athlete, I felt the pain along with them.

Reflections

It never changes when the next one hits. The spectacle of sport at its best is suddenly and violently interrupted. The massive explosion that devastates a city, a government building, takes countless lives and shocks the country. Airplanes that explode in an attempt to bring total chaos to the United States. I am never ready emotionally for the awful feelings that overwhelm me when terrorists strike. And yet I know they will strike again.

MASS MURDERERS

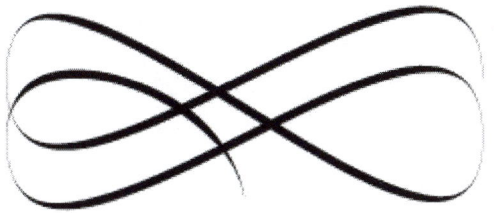

A Flock Of Believers - A Defining Moment

What started out as a man with a purpose to help others, became a drug to him. Jim Jones began a personal ministry in a big city in a vacant church. At first only a few people showed up. But as the flamboyant speaker's message of hope spread amongst the people in the community, more and more began to attend his services. A sense of power took over in his mind; his life. He reveled in the dedication and love of his new "followers". It began to consume him.

He moved his church from the east coast to the warmth of California. All seemed to be going well until certain individuals began leaving the church and complaining to authorities of the strange practices going on behind closed doors. Under extreme scrutiny and financial investigation, Jones moved his operation to South America.

Out of sight, out of mind he thought. Paranoia set in and he warned his followers of impending doom. After a visit from a U.S. senator and his small group's assassination as they were leaving, Jones persuaded the people who worshiped him, that "the evil" was coming. The lines of men, women and children were long to get their glass of poisoned cool aid.

I had stopped in Bedford, Michigan to make a delivery and noticed on their little television on the counter, a breaking news story. A plane was circling the Jonestown compound. Over 460 bodies lying on the ground could be seen from the air.

Later, it was discovered that the adults were lying on top of their children. Over 900 people died that day. I stood there in shock. How could anyone be persuaded to do such a thing; to themselves and especially to their children. To this day, I clearly and sadly remember that moment.

With Evil Charisma

There have been many evil individuals in the world throughout history. In a courtroom, Charles Manson many be #1 in demonic looks. He charmed a small group of women, and then mesmerized them into doing anything he would ask. It became a game to them. But then the game turned deadly.

On a dark night in California, Manson ordered three women to stalk and kill several Hollywood movie stars and industry personnel. When apprehended, the women showed no remorse; only dedication to Manson. When testifying himself, Manson told the judge that society had created what he had become. The look in his eyes was just plain terrifying! With multiple parole hearings, prosecutors vow he'll never get out because he will never be safe in society. He left an eerie impression on me that will never fade.

They Believed - They Followed

David Koresh was well versed in the Biblical scriptures. He was a good looking young man who had charisma and a talent for believable dialogue. He encouraged, corrupted and mesmerized a large group of young, gullible individuals into joining his cult. He claimed to be God and they believed him.

After several defections, and several investigations by authorities, it was decided that the women and children were now in danger. A confrontation came to a head with shooting and then a huge fire that destroyed the Koresh compound. There were no survivors! As I watched on TV; in my mind I thought, how could these precious people have been so misled? It was horrible watching the buildings quickly burn to the ground. All those people gone. All those little children who never had a chance.

Reflections

Nothing makes me cringe more than when an individual can persuade masses of people into believing something that is far from a recognized truth. I remember the hurt in me as I watched on television, the demise of so many believers and their children as they senselessly followed one man's path to destruction.

MASS MURDERS

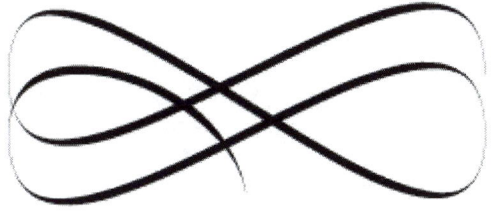

The Evils Of Evil

In all of history, very few catastrophic events can match the evil plan that was Adolph Hitler's in Nazi Germany. He believed the Jews were a disease that needed to be eradicated. And so began one of the most hideous events of the 20th Century and one for all time.

The Jews were marked; separated from their families; loaded onto and packed into railroad box cars like cattle; placed in concentration camps; and systematically tortured, starved, humiliated, decimated and mass annihilated. Their stories are well documented; those stories Must Never Be Forgotten. This horrendous event never again duplicated. 6 million Jews died!

I was born well after the holocaust and World War II. But my study of those events in history have always haunted me. How could a race of people decide that another race different from their own, did not deserve to exist? God will judge all of us someday. But while on earth, it is so difficult to understand the inhumanity that some bring down on others.

The Evil Within

I certainly didn't know him. I wouldn't have wanted to! His ideology was nothing more than a desire to rule; to punish; to have complete control. In Russia during the 20th Century, was a time for absolute authority and anyone who didn't follow the rules, was eliminated.

It is reported that Stalin massacred over 12 million people during his time. When we think of monsters among us, he has to be right there near the top.

There are certain events in history that really bother me. When one man, (or woman), has that much authority to be able to kill at will, it is really unnerving. How could anyone be so callous and without conscious?

Reflections

I often think of the Jewish Holocaust and how utterly horrible it must have been. And most Americans don't even know the horrors of what Joseph Stalin did in Russia. If there has ever been true evil in this world, these two men epitomized it.

EXTRAORDINARY

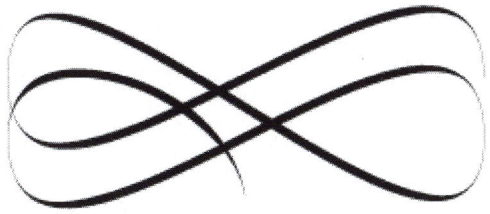

World War II - The Bomb

I was born four years after the war ended. But because I liked history, I was overwhelmed and interested in many facets of this terrible event in human history. The takeover of other countries by Adolph Hitler; his ruthless concentration camps and attempted extermination of the Jews; the sudden attack by Japan on Pearl Harbor, and the terrible loss of life all around the world to conflict.

Over time, I had studied about different aircraft and the improvements each side was making for faster and more destruction capable airships. And then, nearing the end of the war, the Americans developed the first Atomic Bomb.

The first test held many unknowns to it, including how it might affect human beings. Soldiers were stood out in a field to watch the blast. That ended up being immensely cruel and deadly.

With so much at stake, the allies decided it was time. Germany, having already surrendered, left Japan as our focus. We tried to warn them but they were not about to give up their fight. So a single plane with a huge payload, took off and headed for a large city on Japan's mainland.

The first of two deadly bombs exploded over the city and instantly killed thousands; tens of thousands would eventually die from radiation.

Still not willing to surrender, the allies dropped a second bomb on a second city, again doing catastrophic damage and killing a huge number of innocent citizens. The Japanese finally realized their fate, and surrendered. This was a good thing. But the pictures of the devastation and the incredible loss of life just in these two cities alone, was agonizing for me. So far, nuclear weapons have not been used in a conflict. May we pray they never are!

It Was Finally It's Time

The majesty of the mountain in Washington State was breathtaking! Tourists from all walks of life enjoyed the scenic camping areas, even though this mountain was an active volcano. It hadn't erupted in a very long time, but in 1980, there seemed to be signs that just maybe it was waking up.

There were campers and sightseers all around the area when geologists finally convinced park rangers to evacuate the area. The thought of lost revenue by those who ran the campgrounds delayed the initial warnings.

By the time the true rumblings began, for those still in the park, there was no escape. Mount Saint Helens finally exploded, sending fire and ash down the mountain and all around the area.

We human beings just never seem to learn. Mother Nature, in all its beauty, does sometimes send a message that what is natural and will eventually happen – will happen. Quite a few people died that day including a professional photographer. But his camera amazingly survived the blast and those pictures captured the whole incredible event frame by frame. The greed of some, cost others dearly.

Brilliantly Away - Suddenly Gone

The Space Shuttle was a marvel of technology. It allowed us to go into space; travel to the International Space Station, and look out into an incredible universe without hindrance of sight. This was certainly not the first mission, but it was the first for a school teacher. She went through some rigorous training and then on this day, waved to a cheering crowd as she boarded the craft. It was a perfect liftoff and all the indications pointed to the beginning of a successful mission.

I came home that afternoon to my children sitting in the living room watching the TV. It was a newscast showing a video of the liftoff and flight of the shuttle earlier in the day. As I watched, there was suddenly and without warning, an explosion. Something had gone terribly wrong. Later they discovered something in the fuel line on the craft had had a problem.

We will continue venturing into space. We all know that. It's a dangerous and yet rewarding endeavor to scientists. Do we really need to travel into and explore space when we know so little about our own oceans? That unforgettable day will be engrained in my mind forever. The loss of those brave astronauts and passengers will never be forgotten.

Reflections

These three are all so different and yet all have a common denominator. They posed an indelible picture forever in our minds, each with its own cataclysmic boom and an aftershock heard round the world.

The Emptiness Of Our Heart
By Jerry H. Ball
December, 2012

I marked the calendar this day, to say goodbye to something; anything.
Still, as hard as I try, goodbye to it is not enough.
The wrenching, agonizing emptiness keeps engulfing me.

As hard as I try to forget the pain; the loss,
There seems to be no forgetting and the pain persists.
Busyness helps some. Distractions delay.
Occasional smiles from others soothe a little.
But then the busy day is gone –
Not the crummy stuff; the awful emptiness stuff reminds me it's still
there!

Will there come a day when it will be easier
To look in the mirror and not visually see
The pain?
They say it will. But how long will that be?
I will be fair to myself and let my grieving gobble me up
For just now.
But with the help of friends and family and others
Just being nice,
I know it in my heart that it will become easier – less heart wrenching.

I love life, mostly.
My job; my work family; my family family; my good friends
Make this all tolerable.
I know there's a God and I love him.
I did ask him why, and he just didn't answer.
Yet I know He didn't do this,
He just wants me to know that it hurts him too
To see me so sad and hurting.

The sun will come out again for me – I know.
But in the meantime, this really hurts!
Please God, give me the strength I need to make it through each day.

Let me know you're always there, giving me hope.
And let me always be thankful that I could share true love
With such an incredible person, if only for a little while.

ABORTION

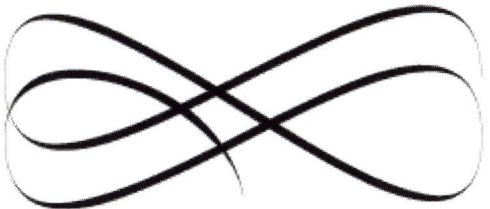

Little Beings - Cruelty And Loss

The abortion issue is one of the most stressful things in my life. To have a human being, there has to be a beginning and that beginning is upon conception. Without conception, there is no baby! The issue has been so complicated in these days of self-absorption, pride and personnel preference. We must stand up for the unborn; to continue to fight to show the world we care about them; that they are all important in God's eyes.

Reflections

For the unborn, my heart aches. It's such a difficult topic and can be controversial within' so many circles. And yet if each of us would look at what each child's possibilities might be, then maybe we would reconsider a decision that for most women is extremely difficult at best and for so many who have gone through the procedure, has extremely traumatic and emotional after effects in their lives.

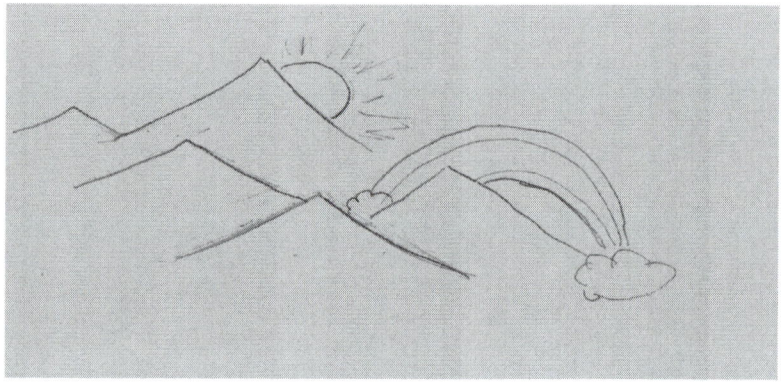

MILITARY

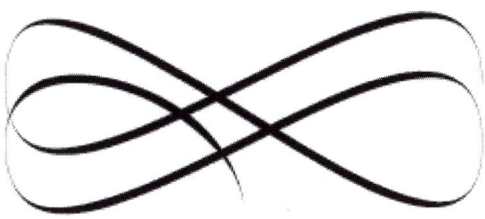

For Love Of Home And Country

As I recently was listening to my favorite Christian radio station and thinking about this book, I was glad that my faith has remained strong; helping me cope with this vast collage of difficult life experiences. And when I turned the channel to a sports broadcast, a man called in who had lost his son in the Afghanistan War in 2013. He was heartbroken and yet very proud of what his son and so many others who have paid the ultimate price, have done to protect our country.

It deeply touched me. The man's voice was so sincere in telling his story, it got me to thinking about my family and our small sacrifices while we served in the military compared to those who have lost their lives. Our service was important. Their service was final!

So what better way to end this book about Sudden Loss than to give my praise, support and hope to all those families and their friends who every day, have to deal with life without their loved one. Freedom is never without a high cost and great sacrifice! May God always be with us in our quest to remain a free nation.

Reflections

I was in the service during the Viet Nam war era from 1970-73. I have nothing but the utmost respect for our military personnel and the difficult job they have to do. And each year on Memorial Day, I remind all those listening to me when I'm in concert, that this day is not just for those who have lost their lives, but it's also for all past service personnel alive today; those still missing, and the ones actively serving at this time. My greatest gratitude goes out to all of our soldiers everywhere serving and protecting our country at this very moment, in this very unstable and sometimes volatile world.

THE BACKPACK - RELIEVED

My backpack is now emptied out. It has been difficult and yet quietly refreshing to unload all of these life affecting moments. I'm glad they are finally out in the open. It is helping me to once and for all, truly deal with them just by thinking about and then writing them down for all to see. What has been a lifetime of my holding them inside, now is a cleansing of my mind, heart and emotions. O' they will still be there in my mind. But now I have lightened the burden that they had become.

I hope that what you have read here may be helpful, insightful and meaningful to you, especially if you also have dealt with Sudden Loss. And if you have, don't hold your emotions in too long. Talk to someone about what you're feeling. I also hope reading these difficult entries were not overwhelming to you. That was absolutely not my purpose in writing this book.

We each deal with Sudden Loss in our own way. Just know that it is helpful in your healing process, if others you know and trust, can go through the mourning and healing process with you.

Sudden Loss is a part of everyone's life. May what I have gone through and lived with all these years become a useful tool in your difficult journey. Thank you so much for sharing this with me.

Jerry

A PARTING THOUGHT

Authors Note:

I love my God, my family, and especially my children and grandchildren. Life is very important to me. I have been so blessed throughout my lifetime with many gifts. I hope to be able to write more often as I believe I have many important issues I want to address in print. And like Sudden Loss, many other subjects of interest are just waiting for me to put them down on paper.

Without the encouragement of many people, I would not be a writer today. This book in particular, is most important to me as it is about a subject we too often want to hide somewhere because it is so hard to deal with. The sudden loss of someone is so mentally, physically and emotionally draining. It takes a tremendous toll on anyone who has experienced it.

I want to thank my immediate family for always encouraging my works; especially my son Kegan. Without him, this project would not be in process and not yet available, as I am unfamiliar with the new wave of publishing techniques that are there via the Internet. My classmates and teachers all through school also deserve credit, as many of them encouraged me as I grew and perfected my craft.

There are so many topics I want to discuss in the future. One is Emotional Sudden Loss. You might say near misses and traumatic events that one experiences and lives to talk about. Another is my experiences with the weather – especially living through multiple tornadoes. Of all of Mother Nature's creations, nothing surpasses what you feel when a funnel cloud announces itself visually and especially audibly.

There is so much to explore in this big world. So to be able to write down what you feel on any topic, is definitely a gift. I am so blessed and privileged to do this. May my days and years ahead allow for many more stories to be written and then to be shared by the world. And to you the reader; thank you for your interest and sharing this time with me.

Jerry

ABOUT THE AUTHOR
(A CHRONOLOGY)

Jerry H. Ball

Father: Joseph L. Ball
Mother: Virginia A. (Cripps) Ball/Converse
Dad: Burl H. Converse (Step Father)

Born March 6, 1949 in Battle Creek, Michigan – Now age 66
Current Residence: Battle Creek, Michigan
Married to Sally Jo Palmiter – March 10, 1990
8 Children: 4 of mine / 1 adopted / 3 step children
Graduated: Delton Kellogg High School – June 1967
Graduated: Kellogg Community College – May 1985
Foster Parent for 29 children / adopted the last one
Drafted into the U.S. Army in December 1970
-          Ft. Dix, New Jersey / Basic Training – Dec. 1970 – Feb. 1971
-          Ft. Gordon, Georgia / A.I.T. – Feb. 1971 – Apr. 1971
-          Augsburg, Germany / Stationed – May 1971 – July 1973
-          Ft. Hood, Texas / Stationed – Aug. 1973 – Dec. 1973
Honorable Discharge
Important Jobs:
          VA Medical Center Battle Creek – 5 years / Engineering
          Battle Creek Fire Dept. – 1981 – 2004 – Retired
          Self Employed House Painting Business – 1987 – Present
          Music Programs / Nursing Homes – 1990 – Present
          Day Care Centers / Special Events
4 Visits To Nashville, Tennessee
Hobbies: Sports (Active and Watch)
Softball, Basketball, Golf, Bowling
Coached All 8 Kids; 4 Grand Children in Baseball
Chess: Played a Chess Master in Germany
Theatre: Plays in H.S., College, Augsburg/Munich, Germany
Church: Hope Church of the Nazarene
Writing:
2 Children's Books; Children's Play; Skits; Poetry; Short Stories
Story Teller for Children
Songwriter: Written Over 80+ Songs
Entertainer: Sing & Play Acoustic Guitar, Accordion & Flute

THE AUTHOR

JERRY H. BALL

BEAUTIFUL DANCER
By Jerry H. Ball

In the moments of forever, now comes the beautiful dancer,
Flowing motion, hard work devotion,
Like gentle breezes, that warm the night,
She is, the beautiful dancer.

With heaven's touching, of a living stage,
A flower in motion, beautiful dancer,
Hard work devotion, discard of notion,
Savior the motion, so pleasing when it's right,
She is, the beautiful dancer.

O' notes of joy, building majestic, magical dance steps,
She takes them in, then gives them back to you and me,
Performing flawlessly,
Sharing beauty in what we see,
She is, the beautiful dancer.

She Is, The Beautiful Dancer.

DULCIE ERIN BALL
BEAUTIFUL DANCER

July 30, 1977 – November 28, 1996

230

DULCIE

By Jerry H. Ball

Where are you now, my little girl,
You seem so far away,
And yet I can feel you inside my heart,
The warmth of your smile fills my days.

The sun that was shining on glossy back roads,
Filled Thanksgiving with joy for a while,
Till' mid-afternoon, when you journeyed afar,
And with you, you carried your smile.

No need to ask why when the answers aren't there,
Just trusting that God is taking good care,
Means that we can go on, and continue on through,
With the sweet loving memories
O' Dulcie that's you.

Of horses and dances and close family,
You made something special of how life should be,
We'll miss you forever, our love do we send,
Till' that special occasion when we'll see you again.

No need to ask why when the answers aren't there,
Just trusting that God is taking good care,
Means that we can go on, and continue on through,
With the sweet loving memories
O' Dulcie that's you.

IN THE MIDDLE OF NOWHERE

By Jerry H. Ball

In the middle of nowhere, where I am,
In the middle of nowhere, where I am,
I don't think that they really understand me,
In the middle of nowhere, where I am.

Taking time to know you,
Taking time to show that you care,
Taking time to know you,
To know you're still there.

We thought the sun would give us time
To live and to grow,
We misused the world we have,
The future we may never know,
I've tried to understand the reasons
We've done what we have done,
Time has passed us by
And we've not cured what we've begun.

In the middle of nowhere, where I am,
In the middle of nowhere, where I am,
I don't think that they really understand me,
In the middle of nowhere, where I am.

Taking time to know you,
Taking time to know that you care,
Taking time to know you,
To know you're still there.

In the middle of nowhere, where I am,
In the middle of nowhere, where I am,
I don't think that I really understand them,
In the middle of nowhere, ------
Where I am.

IT SEEMS THEY LEFT TOO SOON
By Jerry H. Ball

We see you there o' my child my friend,
As though you were held that day,
By an unseen palm, at the cold day's end,
And to you there's still so much to say.

How I miss the children,
It seems so sad they've left this soon,
O' I miss their gentle smiles and laughter,
Children, blessed children.

The beauty and the mountain's majesty,
Cannot prepare you for that unseen hand,
That grasps at time and what's to be,
Within' the Master's secret plan.

How I miss the children,
It seems so sad they've left this soon,
O' I miss their gentle smiles and laughter,
Children, blessed children.

"So quickly gone, the quiet, gentle loves of our hearts and souls,
To leave us longing for their smiles and touches,
And for the little flower petals with their names on them,
That they'd always give so freely,
To those they touched and loved so very much!"

How we miss the children,
It seems so sad they've left this soon,
O' we miss their gentle smiles and laughter,
Children, blessed children.

How we miss the children,
How we miss the children,
It seems they've left too soon.

23096223R00149

Made in the USA
Middletown, DE
17 August 2015